Grow Your Own Vegetables

Grow

Your Own Vegetables

Roger Grounds

VNR VAN NOSTRAND REINHOLD COMPANY
NEW YORK CINCINNATI TORONTO LONDON MELBOURNE

Printed in Spain

Published in 1976 by Van
Nostrand Reinhold Company
A Division of Litton Educational
Publishing. Inc., 450 West 33rd
Street, New York, NY 10001

Van Nostrand Reinhold Limited
1410 Birchmount Road,
Scarborough, Ontario M1P 2E7,
Canada.

Contents

Acknowledgements

No book is ever the work of just one person, however much he would like to think it is, and no matter how original he would like to think his treatment of the subject. Many people have helped me with the preparation of this book and I should like to thank in particular John Ross MacLennan whose idea this book was and who sowed the seeds of the way in which the subject matter has been treated: Ian G. Walls of the West of Scotland Agricultural College for reading the book in manuscript stage and making numerous helpful comments on the practical application of many of the ideas put forward here: and George A. Elbert, author and ex-president of the National Indoor Light Society of America Inc. for his guidance on American vegetable growing practices. The praise is theirs. The rest is mine.

Roger Grounds

Introduction

There is a very old saying, a saying which goes back perhaps to the days when man first cultivated food plants instead of gathering his harvest at random, that there is only one reality, and that is hunger.

If someone had said to you ten—even five—years ago that there would be an acute food shortage within your own lifetime, you would probably not even have bothered to listen. Yet for far longer than that, for fifteen or twenty years, people—serious-minded people like demographers and economists and agronomists—not just the prophets of doom in the popular press—have been warning us all that if we continue to increase our populations without increasing our food production we could face not merely food shortages, but famine.

It is all too easy for those of us who are lucky enough to live in one of the industrio-technological nations of the western world to be complacent about these things. We tend to dismiss famine as something that only happens to other people in faraway places. We take it for granted that there will always be food in the shops: it has all the appearance of being factory-produced, and we buy it in shops just as we buy any other factory-produced item. The reality is different. According to World Health Organisation, 1 person in 8 lives on the sharp edge of starvation. Last year 5,000,000 people did starve to death.

The reasons are many, but man's seemingly irrepressible fecundity has much to do with this crisis. Every second of the day and night the world across, 3 people are born, and only 1 dies. That means that the population of the world is increasing at the rate of 7,500 an hour, 180,000 a day, 66,000,000 a year—equivalent to doubling the 1963 population of the USA every three years. The population of India alone increases by over 1,000,000 people a month—in spite of the fact that in that country alone 12,000 people die of starvation in the same period. The figures are so huge, so horrific one tends to look away. Yet even in the USA, with perhaps the highest standard of living in the world, 2,000 people die of starvation every year. Hunger is not so far from home.

Suddenly the predictions of doom are coming true. Suddenly they are hitting housewife and breadwinner alike. We can no longer take for granted the steady flow of food into the shops. Everytime the house-wife walks into a supermarket something she once took for granted is missing from the shelves. There's a shortage of this or a scarcity of that: panic buying and higher prices. Sugar this year, bananas next year, corn the year after. Who knows?

An acute food shortage is no longer a prediction for the day after tomorrow, or something that happens in faraway lands. It is the reality of today. Tomorrow will be worse.

Yet if you have a patch of land, an eighth of an acre or so, you can grow enough vegetables to keep your family the whole year round. The seeds to start you going will cost little more than you spend on bread in a week, and you'll save enough in a summer to pay for your vacation.

You gain in another way too. The food you grow for yourself will always taste better than anything you buy. And that's not just auto-suggestion. The food you buy in the shops has to measure up to many standards: it has to be the right colour; it has to travel well; it has to last well under supermarket conditions. This limits the varieties grown for commerce. In your own back patch you can grow what you like, all those really tasty vegetables that never reach the shops because they don't travel well or don't store well. The vegetables you grow will be literally garden fresh.

There's another bonus too. If you're worried by all those chemicals they spray on food crops now, at least you'll know what has been used on the vegetables in your own garden. You don't have to use any chemicals if you don't like them.

But there's more to growing your own vegetables than merely saving money or surviving. Though for far too long looked on as the ugly sister to the cultivation of decorative plants, it is in fact one of the most creative and satisfying of all aspects of gardening. Besides, if you spend most of your life bent double over a desk, and most of us do, you'll enjoy the exercise that goes with vegetable gardening, being out in the fresh air, the concentration on a task quite different from your normal routine and the sense of achievement, of a job well done. Good luck.

Part One
1 How to Use This Book

Wherever you are, whoever you are, gardener or beginner, if you want to grow vegetables, this book will tell you just exactly how to do it, and how to do it right. It will start by assuming total ignorance of all gardening matters on your part, and lead you gently, step by logical step, down the garden path, converting you on the way from greenhorn to green thumb.

First of all you need to master Part One. That tells you all the basic essentials. You have got to consider how seriously you want to grow vegetables, whether you want to uproot everything and grow nothing but vegetables, whether you want to give over just a small area, and whether that area is permanent or merely an experimental single season wonder; or whether you want to mix your vegetables in with the decorative plants.

Having decided how much of your land you want to devote to vegetables, it goes on to tell you how to plan that patch of land. It even tells you how to grow vegetables if you haven't got a garden.

Then it tells you about the soil in your garden, what it's made of, why it is the way it is, what plants need from it, and how you can feed your plants and improve the soil all at the same time. However much food there is in the soil for your plants, they can't use any of it without water, so the following chapter discusses water and methods of watering.

Climate is pretty important too. Like the soil, it is one of the factors that limit what you can grow and what you can't. So we tell you quite a bit about climate. But we go one step further. Since you can't change the climate where you live we tell you how to create your own artificial mini-climate, by buying or building a frame or greenhouse.

But there are one or two flies in this utopian ointment: like weeds and bugs and other problems, so we tell you how to deal with them too.

By the time you've read Part I you will have a headful of knowledge. Then all you've got to do is get out into the garden and put it into practice with some real vegetables. That's what Part Two is all about.

So if you follow the instructions set out in this book, you can grow vegetables, whether you knew it or not. You don't even have to be a green thumb to succeed. Just able to read: that's all.

2 Planning

Don't start planning your vegetable garden with a pencil and paper and a grid-sheet like most books tell you.

Go out into your garden and look at it. See how big it is. See what's there already. Make up your mind whether there is already a spare patch of land you could use to grow vegetables. Whether it is worth grabbing another piece of the lawn to make a vegetable garden so that you don't have to disturb the ornamentals, or whether you're going to clear everything out and grow nothing but vegetables. Or are you going to strike a compromise and grow a few vegetables among the ornamentals. It's unorthodox but workable. Use the vegetables instead of the bedding plants and use them in just the same way. These are the sort of decisions you need to make first.

Anyway, how serious are you about growing vegetables? Do you just want to use a small corner of the garden to grow vegetables this season to see if you like it, to see if they are fascinating enough to sustain your interest the season through? Or are you wholly convinced that you want to or need to grow vegetables? And that vegetables are going to be a permanent feature of your garden from now on.

The two groups of decisions are interrelated. Once you have decided how serious you are about growing vegetables, it won't take you long to decide how much of your garden you want to give over to them. Give them as much space as that decision justifies. Then double it.

Now comes the time to reach for your pencil and paper. You do need to know exactly how big your vegetable area is. Unless you know that you simply cannot work out what you have room to grow and what you do not have room to grow. You can make the plan on graph paper if you enjoy that sort of thing, but it is not strictly necessary. What you do need is a plan to scale (otherwise you'll fool yourself into thinking you have more room than you actually have). Take any convenient scale— depending on the size of your garden and the size of your piece of paper: 1 yard = 1 inch is quite convenient, or 1 metre = 1 centimetre. Show on the plan only the perimeter of the vegetable area. You have more decisions to make before you can determine how you want to divide it up into plots. Also mark on your plan where north is.

The next thing to do is make a list on a separate sheet of paper of the vegetables you think you would like to grow, and then find out whether you can in fact grow them in your area. Unfortunately most of the information you need in order to determine that is contained in chapters you have not yet read. However, much of it is summarised in the **Planting Chart**. If you take one of the vegetables on your hypothetical list and look it up on the **Planting Chart**, these are the factors you have to determine.

Soil
Not mentioned on the chart, but dealt with fully in the chapter 'Know Your Soil'. Most vegetables will tolerate a very wide range of soils, so for simplicity let's assume that your soil is right for the vegetable. However, if your soil is either heavy clay or bedrock you will have to grow your vegetables in artificial raised beds. Then you will need to decide whether the beds are to be permanent or movable.

Hardiness
This is dealt with fully in the chapters 'Climate' and 'Artificial Climates'. Briefly, a vegetable will be Hardy, Half-hardy or Tender. Once you know which it is, turn to the zone maps. These divide the USA and the UK into 3 hardiness zones—Hardy, Half-hardy and Tender. Where the name's the same you can grow that vegetable out of doors. If it is one zone warmer you will need to start it under glass to plant out for the summer. How you do that is explained in the chapter 'Artificial Climates'. If it is two zones warmer you need to grow it under glass all the year, and you'll find all you need to know about that in the same chapter. To keep things moving let's assume you can grow the vegetable you are using as a dummy run out of doors.

Number of Growing Days
Most American readers will be familiar with this concept, but few British readers will. 'Number of Growing Days' means the number of days the crop needs to be in the ground from the time you sow the seed till the time you start to harvest. For the most part, growing days are frost-free days (exceptions are specifically mentioned in the text). Having found the number of growing days your vegetable needs, turn up the Last Frost Map, which gives you the date of your last frost and the number of growing days; find the town nearest the area you live in. If the number of growing days for your area is less than the number of growing days needed by your vegetable, you will not be able to grow it. For example, if you live in Errol, New Hampshire, and only have 96 growing days, you won't be able to grow onions from seed because they need between 100 and 165 days to mature. You have the same problem if you live in the Highlands of Scotland where your last frost is 1 June and your first frost is 15 August, giving only 77 growing

days. Again, you can use some of the techniques discussed in the chapter 'Artificial Climates' to overcome this shortfall.

These three factors, Soil, Hardiness and Growing days determine whether or not you can grow any particular vegetable in your area. Assuming you can, the next group of decisions to be made concerns the amount of space you are going to have to devote to each vegetable.

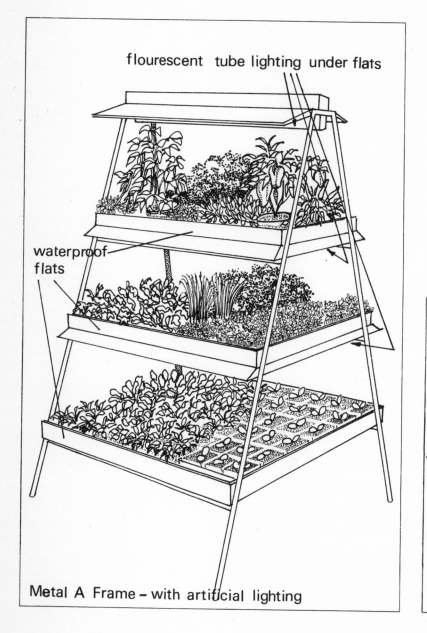

flourescent tube lighting under flats

waterproof flats

Metal A Frame – with artificial lighting

Mobile A Frame – to catch the sun

In order to work this out, first look up the number of 'Plants per Person' column. This is not a spot-accurate figure, merely an average, based on what the average person eats in the average season. Tastes and eating habits vary from person to person, and no one is average, but it is a good starting figure: keep your own records and see if you need to grow more or less next year. Obviously if you plan to freeze or dry the vegetables, you can increase the quantities—probably double them in most cases. Since the figure is for one average person, to work out what you need for your family just multiply by the number of people in your family.

You now know the number of plants you want to grow this year. Look up the 'distance between plants' column and work out how long a row you would need assuming you put all your plants in a straight row. The rows, incidentally, should run north/south to catch most sun and develop evenly. For example: if you need 4 plants per person and there are five of you in your family, you're going to need 20 plants for the season. If the plants need to be 3 ft/1 m apart, then you will need a single row of plants 60 ft/20 m long (20 × 3). However, if you only have room to have rows 15 ft/5 m long you are going to need 4 rows. To find out how much room they'll take up you just look up the 'distance between rows' column. Assuming the distance between rows is 3 ft/1 m, you're going to need 12 ft/4 m to accommodate your 4 rows (3 × 4). That means you need an area 15 ft by 12 ft/5 m × 4 m to produce your family's needs of that vegetable.

You may well find that the area needed for the vegetable you have chosen will occupy the whole of your garden. Don't be discouraged. Work through a few more examples from your priorities list till you find what you can fit into your garden. Work all the permutations to see how best you can fit them in.

The 'Seeds per Foot' column tells you how many seeds you need to sow per foot in order to obtain the number of plants you want (plants per foot). It allows for a few to fail to come up, or get eaten by bugs. Never be tempted to grow the plants closer together than the recommended distances. You'll get less plants, not more. Waste a couple of plants and prove it for yourself. Let two lettuce seedlings grow on side by side. You won't finish up with two well-formed lettuces, each with a good firm heart. You'll finish up with two malformed lettuces that have failed to heart properly, and you'll probably decide both of them are not fit to serve up, so you'll throw them into the compost bin. The distances recommended will give you the best crops, so stick to them.

Work out the space required by all the vegetables you want to grow for your family, then trim your ambitions to the ground available.

Try to see how you are going to lay them out on the ground. Do rough sketches first, then try the thing to scale. This is where graph paper really can come in handy. Cut out pieces of paper to scale representing the area each crop will occupy, label them with the name of the

Raised Bed System - showing different bed heights

crop or colour-code them (red for tomatoes, green for peas and so on or whatever colours you fancy—but keep a key to your colour code) then shuffle the pieces of paper round on a plan of the vegetable area drawn to the same scale. That way you can find out quickly how best to combine crops to get the maximum yield from the land available. In general, short rows are easier to work than long rows, so if, for example, you have a long narrow patch of land, have a central path with the rows going off at right angles to it, rather than long rows running parallel with the path.

Then there's the problem of what to do with the weeds you pull out and trimmings from the plants, not to mention the throw-away parts you can't eat or cook. So you need to plan an area for a series of compost bins. Also a bonfire, in areas where these are allowed. Bonfire ash is rich in plant foods that encourage firm growth and good colour.

Paths can be a headache too. Rather than just trample the mud down along your main traffic lanes, lay yourself a proper path of bricks, concrete, cobbles or paving slabs. Or use gravel or chippings. But if you use these you need to edge the bed properly, otherwise the gravel or chippings will work their way into the soil of the vegetable plot, while the soil will get mixed up with the gravel or chippings. For the path to be much use to you it needs to be 3 ft/1 m wide.

For edgings use old-fashioned kitchen garden edging tiles if you can get them. If you can't, use bricks laid dog-tooth fashion, or large planks of pressure-treated seasoned hardwood. If you want to have raised beds you can build these with bricks, or use old railroad ties.

When you've got your first season's plan worked out, put it on a clipboard and put the year at the head of it. Keep it. Each year place the following year's plan on top of it. This way you know how you are rotating your crops. If you want to keep records too, keep them on another clipboard and keep the two together. The sort of records you might want to keep are first and last frost records. Maps of this sort of thing are helpful, but they are based on figures averaged out for an area. You may be in a tiny little mild pocket (or a tiny little cold pocket) missed out in the averaging-out process. You might also want to keep records of crop yields so that you can compare them with weather records. See what effect a late spring or an extra hot summer has on the yield. Also keep records of fertilisers used to see which give the best results on your soil. This way you'll learn things no book will ever tell

Raised Bed with plank edging – do all your gardening sitting down

you. How can it? It's painting pictures on too broad a canvas—only you can fill in the details. Ultimately you will be absolute master or mistress of your own vegetable patch. However, this is an extra, a luxury for the really keen vegetable grower.

You can grow perfectly good vegetables by following the instructions in this or any other book. The facts and figures are as accurate as possible, but they are not absolute and they are not critical. Vegetables are the most tolerant of all plants. They won't mind too much if you plant them a little too early or a little too late. So use the facts and figures here as a starting point. Then adjust them to suit your own garden. Watch the plants and let them tell you whether you are planting them too late or too early, too many or too few.

Lastly, take a pride in your vegetable patch. Keep it spick and span,

	HARDINESS	pH IDEAL	SOWING DEPTH	SOWING TIME	SEEDS PER FOOT	DAYS TO GERMINATION	% GERMINATION	WHEN TO TRANSPLANT
Asparagus	Hardy	6·5	$1\frac{1}{2}$ in	2 weeks after last frost	Random	7–21	70	1 week after last frost
Beans, Butter, Lima or Madagascar	Tender	6·0	$1\frac{1}{2}$ in	4 weeks after last frost	Bush 5–8 Pole 4–5	7–12	70	6 weeks after last frost
Beans, English, Broad or Fava	Hardy	6·2	$2\frac{1}{2}$ in	November for spring crop in H-H areas. 4 weeks before last frost for early summer crop	5–8	7–14	75	—
Beans, Runner	Half-hardy	6·2	2–3 in	3 weeks after last frost	4–6	6–14	75	2 weeks after last frost
Beans, Snap, French, Kidney or String	Tender	6·8	$1\frac{1}{2}$ in	8 weeks after last frost. 6 weeks earlier under glass	6–8	6–14	80+	8 weeks after last frost
Beets	Half-hardy	6·5	1 in	Last frost date. Under cloches, 5 weeks earlier	10–15	7–14	60+	—
Broccoli	Half-hardy	6·5	$\frac{1}{2}$ in	3 weeks after last frost	10–15	7–12	75+	4 weeks after last frost
Brussels Sprouts	Hardy	6·2	$\frac{1}{2}$ in	2 weeks after last frost and/or June/July	10–15	7–12	75+	2 weeks after last frost and/or July/August
Cabbage	Hardy	6·5	$\frac{1}{2}$ in	Summer harvest: 6 weeks before transplant. Fall/winter: 4, 8, 12 weeks after last frost	8–10	7–12	75+	2–8 weeks after last frost

weed-free and clear from trimmings. Keep it looking as though at any moment the man who hands out the prizes for the world's best-kept vegetable garden might drop in on you. Not just for appearance's sake, but because the vegetables will grow better if you look after the whole area that well. Whatever you do, don't let it get into a run-down state of pernicious perennial weeds popping up here and there among discarded vegetable stalks. That encourages bugs and other infestations, apart from looking hideous.

SPACE BETWEEN PLANTS	SPACE BETWEEN ROWS	YIELD PER PLANT	PLANTS PER PERSON	DAYS TO HARVEST	LIFE OF SEED	VARIETIES
8 in	36 in	1½ lbs	10	3 years	2 years	'Connover's Colossal', 'Mary Washington', 'Purple Argenteuil', 'Waltham Washington'
Bush: 3–6 in Pole: 6–10 in	Bush: 24–30 in Pole: 30–36 in	2 oz	48	90–100	3 years	Bush: 'Fordhook 242', Comtesse de Chambord, Henderson Bush', 'Thaxter'. Pole: 'Goliath' (Prizetaker), 'King of the Garden', 'Challenger'
4 in	18–24 in	2 oz	48	80–90	3 years	Bush: 'The Midget'. Pole: Early: 'Aquadulce'. Late: 'Imperial Green Longpod', 'Imperial White Longpod'
6 in	36–48 in	2 lbs	10	60–70	3 years	Bush: 'Brezo', 'Hammonds' Dwarf Scarlet'. Pole: 'Achievement', 'Enorma', 'Prizewinner', 'Streamline'
Bush: 2–3 in Pole: 4–6 in	Bush: 18–30 in Pole: 36–48 in	1 oz	56	60–80	3 years	Bush: 'Bush Blue Lake', 'Canadian Wonder', 'Devil Fin Precoce', 'Golden Waxpod', 'Romano 14', 'Royalty', 'Tendercrop'. Pole: 'Blue Lake', 'Kentucky Wonder', 'Romano', 'Stringless'
in	12–18 in	8 oz	48	50–70	4 years	Rootcrop: 'Boltardy', 'Cheltenham Greentop', 'Burpees Golden', 'Early Wonder', 'Mono-king Explorer', 'Ruby Queen'. For Greens: 'Green Fop Bunching', 'Lutz Green Leaf', 'Sugar Beet', 'White Beet'
4–18 in	24–30 in	12–16 oz	5	60–100	3 years	'Calabrese', 'Green Comet', 'Green Sprouting', 'Waltham 29'
2–18 in	24–30 in	1 lb 4 oz	5	100–110	5 years	'Achilles', 'Jade Cross', 'King Arthur', 'Long Island Improved', Peer Gynt', 'Topscore'
2–20 in	24–30 in	1 lb 8 oz	5	60–150	4 years	Summer Harvest: 'Avoncrest', 'Golden Acre', 'Green Express', 'Greyhound', 'Primo', 'Red Acre'. Fall & Winter Harvest: 'Celtic', 'Chieftain Savoy', 'Early Head', 'January king', 'Savoy king', 'Winter Monarch'

	HARDINESS	pH IDEAL	SOWING DEPTH	SOWING TIME	SEEDS PER FOOT	DAYS TO GERMINATION	% GERMINATION	WHEN TO TRANSPLANT
Carrots	Hardy	6·0	$\frac{1}{4}$ in	Last frost date. Again in July for fall crop	15–20	10–21	50+	—
Cauliflower	Half-hardy	6·5	$\frac{1}{2}$ in	Indoors: 6 weeks before transplant. Outdoors: 2 weeks after last frost	8–10	7–12	75+	Last frost date
Celery	Half-hardy	6·8	$\frac{1}{4}$ in	10–12 weeks before transplant date	8–12	10–30	55	6 weeks after l frost
Corn	Tender	6·5	2 in	Indoors: 10–12 weeks before transplant date	4–6	6–12	75+	4–6 weeks afte last frost
Cucumber	Tender	7·0	1 in	4–6 weeks before transplant date	3–5	6–14	80+	4 weeks after l frost
Eggplant, Aubergine	Tender	5·5	$\frac{1}{2}$ in	Outdoors: 4 weeks after last frost. Indoors: 7–10 weeks before transplant date	8–12	7–14	60	4 weeks after l frost
Kale	Hardy	6·5	$\frac{1}{2}$ in	3–4 months before first frost	8–10	7–12	75+	4 weeks before last frost
Kohlrabi	Half-hardy	6·5	$\frac{1}{2}$ in	Outdoors: last frost date. Indoors: 4–6 weeks earlier	8–12	3–14	75	1 week after la frost
Leeks	Hardy	6·5	1 in	Outdoors: 4 weeks before last frost. Indoors: 8–12 weeks earlier	8–12	7–14	75+	6 weeks after l frost
Lettuce	Half-hardy	7·5	$\frac{1}{2}$ in	2 weeks after last frost, then at 2 week intervals till midsummer	Head: 4–8 Leaf: 8–12	4–12	80+	4 weeks after la frost
Marrows and Squashes	Half-hardy	6·5	1 in	Outdoors: 4–6 weeks after last frost. Indoors: 3–4 weeks earlier	Summer: 4–6 Winter: 1–2	Summer: 5–14 Winter: 6–12	75+	4–6 weeks afte last frost
Melons (Cantaloupes)	Half-hardy	6·0	1 in	Outdoors: 4–6 weeks after last frost (USA only). Indoors: 3–4 weeks earlier	3–6	4–12	70+	4–6 weeks afte last frost
Onion	Hardy	6·0	$\frac{1}{2}$ in	Outdoors: last frost date. Indoors: 8 weeks earlier than outdoors	10–15	7–14	70+	1 week after las frost date

SPACE BETWEEN PLANTS	SPACE BETWEEN ROWS	YIELD PER PLANT	PLANTS PER PERSON	DAYS TO HARVEST	LIFE OF SEED	VARIETIES
–2 in	18–24 in	1–2 oz	120	60–85	3 years	'Autumn king', 'Coreless', 'Nantes', 'Red Cored Chantenay'
8 in	30–36 in	10 lbs	5	60–100	4 years	'All the Year Round', 'Asmer Snocap', 'Polar Bear', 'Snowball', 'Snow king'
in	24–30 in	3 lbs	7	100–140	5 years	'Golden Self-Blanching', 'Greenstick', 'Summer Pascal'
–14 in	30–36 in	1 ear	20	60–100	3 years	'Golden Bantam', 'Northern Belle', 'Polar Vee', 'Silver Queen', 'Snow Cross', 'Sprite'
in or 3 plants per hill	48–72 in or 5 ft between hills	4 lbs	4–6	55–75	5 years	Slicing: 'Ashley', 'Burpee Hybrid', 'Burpless Green king', 'Marketmore', 'Triumph Hybrid'. Pickling: 'SMR 48', 'Pioneer'
4–36 in	48 in	7 lbs	5	80–90	5 years	'Black Beauty', 'Burpee Hybrid', 'Early Beauty', 'Jersey king'
–12 in	18–24 in	1 lb	6	55–65	5 years	'Blue Curled Scotch', 'Dwarf Green Curled', 'Dwarf Siberian Curled'
–6 in	18–24 in	7 oz	20	60–75	5 years	'Early Purple Vienna', 'Early White Vienna'
–4 in	12–18 in	8 oz	24	80–90 from sets 130–150 from seed	3 years/ sets overwinter	'Everest', 'Large American Flag', Malabar, 'Marble Pillar', 'Yates Empire'
Head: 2–14 in Leaf: 4–6 in	Head: 18–24 in Leaf: 12–18 in	12 oz	5 per planting	45–80	6 years	Head: 'Avoncrisp', 'Great Lakes'—Crisphead. 'Webbs Wonderful', 'Buttercrunch', 'Arctic king', 'Iceberg'—Butterhead. Leaf: 'Salad Bowl', 'Grand Rapids', 'Oak Leaf'—Leaf or Bunching. 'Dark Green Cos', 'Paris Island Cos', 'Histon Crispie', 'Little Gem', 'Green Cos'—Cos
Summer: 4–24 in Winter: 4–48 in	Summer: 36–60 in Winter: 72–120 in	Summer: 4 lbs Winter: 3 lbs	Summer: 2 Winter: 3	Summer: 50–60 Winter: 80–120	4 years	Summer: 'Early Prolific Straightneck', 'Hubbard Golden', 'Sweet Dumpling', 'Vegetable Spaghetti', 'Zucchmann'. Winter: 'Butternut', 'Hundredweight', 'Gold Nugget'
2–16 in	60–72 in	25–30 lbs	5–15	75–100	2 years	'Burpee Hybrid', 'Early Crenshaw', 'Gold Star', 'Ieognois'
–3 in	12–24 in	4 oz	15	100–165	1 year	Short Day (12 hours) (Southern USA): 'Excel', 'Texas Grano', 'Crystal Whitewax', 'Yellow Bermuda'. Long Day (14–16 hours) (UK & Northern USA): 'Bunching Onions', 'Scallions', 'Early Yellow', 'Sweet Spanish', 'Ailsa Craig', 'White Lisbon'

	HARDINESS	pH IDEAL	SOWING DEPTH	SOWING TIME	SEEDS PER FOOT	DAYS TO GERMINATION	% GERMINATION	WHEN TO TRANSPLANT
Peas (English, Edible podded, Snow or Sugar)	Hardy	7·0	2 in	Last frost date	6–7	6–15	80+	—
Peppers, Sweet and Hot	Tender	6·5	$\frac{1}{4}$ in	Indoors: 8 weeks earlier than outdoors: 4 weeks after last frost	6–8	10–25	55	5 weeks after last frost
Potato, White	Half-hardy	5·5	4 in	2 weeks before last frost		7–21	95+	—
Pumpkins	Tender	7·0	1$\frac{1}{2}$ in	Outdoors: 4–6 weeks after last frost. Indoors: 3–4 weeks after last frost	2	6–14	70	4–6 weeks after last frost
Radish	Hardy	7·0	$\frac{1}{2}$ in	Last frost date then every 2 weeks till 1 August	14–16	3–14	75+	—
Shallots	Hardy	6·0	1 in	Last frost date	8–12	7–14	60	Last frost date
Spinach	Hardy	6·5	$\frac{1}{2}$ in	Hardy areas: 4 weeks before last frost. Half-hardy and tender areas: 1 October thro' 1 March	10–12	6–14	60+	—
Swiss Chard (Seakale Beet)	Half-hardy	6·5	1 in	Last frost date then at 2 week intervals till July/August	6–10	7–14	65	—
Tomato	Tender	4·0	$\frac{1}{2}$ in	Outdoors: 4 weeks after last frost. Indoors: 5–7 weeks earlier	Random	7–14	75+	4–6 weeks after last frost

SPACE BETWEEN PLANTS	SPACE BETWEEN ROWS	YIELD PER PLANT	PLANTS PER PERSON	DAYS TO HARVEST	LIFE OF SEED	VARIETIES
2–3 in	18–24 in	1 lb	250–300	65–90	3 years	'Alaska', 'Little Marvel', 'Burpee Sweetpod', 'Mammoth Melting Sugar', 'Yates Fortune', 'Kelvedon Wonder', 'Onward', 'Achievement'
18–24 in	24–36 in	1½–2 lbs	4	100–120	2 years	Sweet: 'Bell Boy', 'Keystone Resistant Giant', 'Yolo Wonder', 'Fordhook', 'Ruby King', 'California Wonder'. Hot: 'Long Red Cayenne', 'Tabasco', 'Hungarian Wax', 'Hungarian Yellow Wax'
12 in	24–36 in	6–8 lbs	25–30	90–120	Overwinter	Early: 'Arran Pilot', 'Irish Cobbler', 'Craig's Royal', 'Norchip'. Maincrop: 'Kemebec', 'King Edward VII', 'Arran Victory', 'Dr. McIntosh', 'Katahedin'
30–36 in	70–120 in	3–5 pumpkins (20–30 lbs each)	3	75–150	4 years	'Big Tom' ('Connectiant Field'), 'Cinderella', 'Small Sugar' (New England Pie), 'Big Max' (the 100 lbs pumpkin), 'Cheyenne Bush'
1–2 in	6–12 in	1–1½ oz	30 per sowing	20–60	4 years	'Cherry Belle', 'Rota', 'French Breakfast', 'White Icicle'
2–4 in	12–18 in	8 oz	15	60–75	1 year	'Dutch Yellow', 'Giant Red'
2–4 in	12–18 in	8 oz	5 per planting	40–70	3 years	Longstanding Varieties—plant Spring: 'America', 'Writer Bloomsdale', 'Long Standing Bloomsdale', 'Giant Thick Leaved'. Shortstanding—fall & winter: 'Hybrid No. 7', 'Dixie Market', 'Dynamo', 'Viking'
4–8 in	18–24 in	10 oz	5 per planting	55–75	4 years	'Lucullus', 'Ruby Chard', 'Rhubarb Chard', 'Fordhook Giant'
18–36 in	36–60 in	10–12 lbs	5	55–110	4 years	Hardy Areas: 'Moneymaker', 'Ailsa Craig', 'Eurocross', 'Maascross', 'Extase', 'Supersonic', 'Jet Star', 'Spring Set'. Half-Hardy Areas: 'Homestead', 'Rutgers', 'Manalucie', 'Floradel'

3 So Your Garden's Too Small?

Don't for a moment imagine that you can't grow vegetables just because your garden's too small, or because your garden hasn't got a good, deep loamy soil. Anyone can grow vegetables. If they want to. Indoors or out. If your backyard's too full of precious plants, take a hole out of the lawn in front of the house, grow a ring of beets surrounded by a ring of carrots or chives. Tell your visitors it's only decorative. But it supplements the diet. Use your ingenuity.

Here are some of the problem conditions, and some of the options open to you.

Poor Soil

A good soil in which to grow vegetables is deep and easily worked. Many gardeners have to be content with difficult soils, and you may be one of them. Maybe your garden seems to be made up of nothing but stones: or maybe you're gardening on bedrock or hardpan, or on heavy clay that just won't drain: or on almost pure sand where all the water drains away before the plants have had time to have a drink.

The easiest answer here is quite simply not to garden in the soil. Instead, garden on top of it.

This means making raised beds. If you raise the beds you have got to find some way to hold the soil in place, otherwise it will scatter, and the beds will dry out round the edges. So, if you're thinking of raised beds, the first thing to do is to decide whether the beds are to be permanent or temporary. If the beds are going to be permanent then build up the edges with brick, faced stone, railway ties (their heaviness entitles these to be considered permanent), or pre-shaped concrete blocks. (If you're a handyman you can design and make your own concrete blocks.) If you use brick, stone or concrete you're going to need a foundation, otherwise your wall will bend and twist with extremes of weather and finally fall over. Foundations should be dug 4 in/10 cm deep and 9 in/23 cm wide for a wall 12 in/30 cm high. Add 1 in/2·5 cm in depth for every foot/30 cm higher you want the wall.

For less permanent structures use wood, preferably hardwood that has been pressure-treated with preservative. The simplest type of

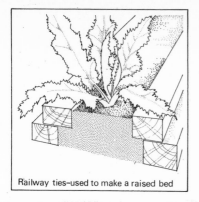

Railway ties–used to make a raised bed

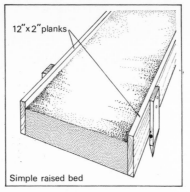

12"x 2" planks

Simple raised bed

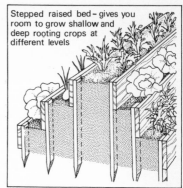

Stepped raised bed – gives you room to grow shallow and deep rooting crops at different levels

wood raised bed is one made of planks 12 in by 2 in/30 cm by 5 cm, with hardwood stakes nailed or screwed to them to hold them upright. The stakes should penetrate at least 12 in/30 cm into the ground.

The size of the beds, unless it has already been determined for you by the size of your garden, depends entirely upon whether you want to weed from both sides or from one side only. If you can weed from both sides, then an ideal size for the bed is from 6–8 ft/2–2·5 m. It can be as long as you like. With raised beds this width you can carry out all cultural operations—seeding, planting, weeding and harvesting—without having to walk on the bed. If you make the bed wider you will need to walk on it, in which case you need to place 12 in by 4 in/30 by 10 cm planks across the beds. Walk on these: it saves compacting the soil.

If you only have access to the bed from one side (because it is against a wall or a fence or the house) keep it no more than 3–4 ft/1–1·2 m wide. Further than that you cannot reasonably reach without having to put a hand or a foot on the bed.

If you're going to have a raised bed at all, you need to raise the soil inside it by at least 12 in/30 cm to give the plants plenty of depth for their roots. If you treasure your own comfort too, raise the bed to 16 or 18 in/40–46 cm, then put a 6 in/15 cm plank round the edge, so you can sit while you weed.

If you make raised beds in the way just described you will find they are big enough to grow any of the vegetables mentioned in this book. However, if you have a smaller garden and want to concentrate on the smaller vegetables, try this idea.

Start with a raised bed, made as described above, but only 3 ft/1 m wide, and with planks only 6 in/15 cm high. Fill with soil or growing mix and level. Then, 6 in/15 cm inside the outer planks, raise another bed 6 in/15 cm above the level of the soil. Use 6 in/15 cm planks for this, but remember to make the holding stakes an extra 6 in/15 cm long to take account of the already raised soil. Fill with compost of growing mix and then add a central raised bed 6 in/15 cm above that and 6 in/15 cm in from your second tier. This central bed will be 1 ft/30 cm wide, while the two tiers below only 6 in/15 cm wide. Use the wide, deep central bed for your larger growing vegetables, the outer ones for smaller vegetables like radishes and carrots, perhaps some dwarf bush beans or, if you use a rich soil mix, cucumbers that can trail over the edge.

Those are the principles, the main guidelines, but there are many variations on the theme. You can work out your own permutations. But it is worth remembering that it often pays, if you have raised beds at all, to have them raised on two levels, even if it doesn't seem necessary to start with. There's a very good reason for this. The soil in raised beds warms up quicker in spring than the soil in the surrounding ground. The soil in a bed raised 18 or even 24 in/46 or 60 cm warms up more quickly than soil in a bed raised only 6 in/15 cm or a foot/30 cm. The difference can be substantial, as much as 2, 3 or even 4 weeks, depending on which zone you live in. This early warming of the soil means that you can plant in these raised beds that many weeks before you could put seed in the ground. Use this advantage to grow extra early crops, for crops where an early start means you can grow two lots in a season instead of one, or for long season crops. Use them also for rootcrops that like a deep soil.

In fact, raised beds are such a good idea that many gardeners whose soil is rich and friable, use them too. They do this partly to get an earlier start in the growing season, but also because raised beds are easier to maintain, look smarter, neater, tidier. That in turn encourages you to keep them looking smarter, tidier and weed-free.

No Soil
Obviously this can be a problem so long as you pursue traditional modes of thinking. Plants, all plants, even so-called 'air plants' need something to grow in.

So if you've got a backyard put down to concrete (and plenty of people have: it saves weeding!), or a beautifully paved patio, a roof garden, a balcony, a deck outside a hillside home or just the platform at the back of a mobile home, you've got problems. According to traditional thinking you've got only two options: break up the concrete or paving till you find the soil, or forget vegetable growing.

Don't forget it. Start thinking. If you're gardening at ground level all you've got to do is put raised beds down on the concrete or paving. Don't bother with the holding stakes: it's hell trying to get them through concrete: use tie bars instead to hold the sides equal distances apart. Fill them with compost or growing mix: use soil if you can get some. If you're gardening anywhere other than at ground level, don't use soil: use lightweight soilless growing mixes.

There are other options open to you too. Most of them are based on the principle of flats or seed-trays—but jumbo-sized. You need roughly a 6 in/15 cm depth of soil to succeed with any vegetable: if you can make it deeper so much the better. Here's the simplest idea of all.

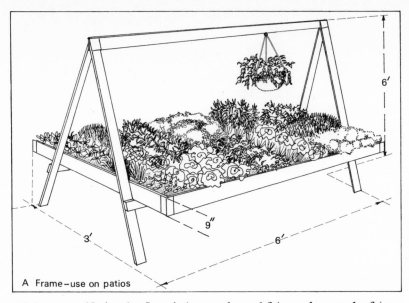

A Frame—use on patios

Make yourself a jumbo flat 9 in/23 cm deep, 6 ft/12 m long and 3 ft/1 m wide. Use hardwood planks 1 in by 6 in/2·5 cm by 15 cm. Then make a sawhorse 6 ft/2 m high, with transverse parallel bars to carry the jumbo flat. If you can, use metal angle-irons on the corners: it makes the job last longer. When you've made it, it's called an A-frame. Look at it end on and you'll see why. Divide the flat into 3 or 4 parts with cross members: these not only give you the means of tying the sides together securely, and keeping the bottom attached to the flat, but they mean that you can clearly separate one crop from another, and use different soils in different sections if you want to. You can even rotate your crops if you make the structure relatively permanent. You can put the saw horse on wheels and move it round to follow the sun. That's an advantage your fixed-bed gardeners don't have. Usually you'll find it more convenient to throw the soil away and fold the whole thing flat and store it over winter.

When using the A-frame or any other garden which is basically a box, there are two important things to remember. The first is that you must provide adequate drainage. This means drilling not less than 5 quarter-inch/6 mm holes in each sq ft/30 cm² of bottom. The other is to crock the bottom, otherwise the soil or growing mix will quickly block the drain holes.

There are many variants on this jumbo flats idea. Two particularly useful ones are these. One is to set the flats on legs, which should be not less than 2 by 2 in/5 by 5 cm square, and not more than 3 ft/1 m apart, screwed securely into the sides of the flats: alternatively you can make benching and simply put the flats on top of this. You can then replace any flats that deteriorate without having to remake the whole system.

Raised Jumbo Flats – perfect for the disabled

Arrange the flats in whatever shape makes them most convenient to cultivate. If you arrange them in the sort of shape a computer writes the letter C, you have easy access and can cultivate the whole lot from the middle. If you make the legs 33 in/83 cm high you'll find the beds can be worked conveniently from a chair: or from a wheelchair— particularly useful for the disabled.

Another method is to fix the flats to tripods. Not the sort of tripod you stand a camera on: on that the three legs come together at the top. You want a tripod with all three legs parallel. And preferably two sets of tripods for stability. One of the legs can double-up, being part of both tripods, so that you end up with 3 legs on one side and 2 on the other. If you've got room, make the poles 10 ft/3·2 m tall, place the flats about 2½–3 ft/46–92 cm up them, and then you can grow pole beans or scarlet runners up them. Place netting or strings between the up-

Jumbo Flat on Tripod – for lawns

X Frame optimises space in small gardens

rights and you can grow melons, squashes, cucumbers and tomatoes up them. For ease of cultivation, keep the tallest crops in the middle. It looks better that way too.

A real space-saver for anyone without a garden is a stair-step garden. This is made of a series of boxes, just like windowboxes, say 6 in/15 cm deep, 6 in/15 cm wide and 4 ft/1·2 m long, plus one box 12 in/30 cm wide but still 6 in/15 cm deep and 4 ft/1·2 m long securely screwed to either an X- or an A-frame at each end. The biggest box goes at the top, and grows the biggest vegetables, while the six other boxes are ranged in stepped threes down each side. Orient the box north/south so that the boxes on both sides get sun. Don't forget the drain-holes, and don't forget the lightweight growing mix if you are using the frame on a rooftop or balcony.

Container Growing
The flats already mentioned are just one type of container. There are dozens of other types of containers you can use for growing vegetables when you are pushed for space or lack soil. You can buy giant flower pots—up to 4 ft/1·2 m in diameter—in clay or plastic: you can buy strawberry pots, plastic, fibreglass or reconstituted stone tubs, urns and so on, even lead troughs or good imitations of them if you want to. They're all useful, and they're all expensive.

There are dozens of other throw-away things you can use if you have a mind to. Kipper boxes, potato baskets, half-barrels, tubs, grape baskets, even old buckets, wheelbarrows or garden trailers. If it's big enough to hold some soil, then it's big enough to grow vegetables in. Anything you think is a bit on the fragile side, fill with lightweight soilless growing mix, not earth.

Take a half-tub and think what you could do with it. You could make a salad bowl out of it. Put a clump of chives in the middle, round

Use half-tubs for Pole Beans
or Squashes

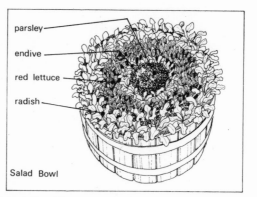

parsley
endive
red lettuce
radish

Salad Bowl

them a ring of radishes, then a ring of red lettuce or one of the miniature lettuces, then endive. Or fill it with really rich compost and grow cucumbers or melons: let them trail all over the place. Or put a pole in the middle, tie strings at equal distances all round the rim and up to the top of the pole and grow pole beans or scarlet runners up the strings. Or tomatoes. Keep trying and you'll find many more ways of using this one half-tub year by year.

Once you become dedicated to vegetables, use the tubs for good-looking vegetables, especially those with colourful fruits—eggplants, tomatoes, squashes. They'll thrive in containers, especially as there's less temptation to plant them out too early.

Use Your Ingenuity

If you want to grow vegetables and you're short of space, don't just use any one of these ideas: use the lot, and many more. Orient yourself to thinking 'How can I use that space?' You'll soon find yourself full of ideas. Here are some more.

Don't just settle for an A-frame or a range of flats on legs, but combine both, and have some tubs as well: have a tripod in another corner. Use a strawberry pot or barrel to grow strawberries or peas from the holes in the sides, and the top for a vine such as cucumber, melon, tomato, trained along a plastic mesh trellis on a wall or fence. If you've got room, have half a dozen pots, each with a vine growing into the

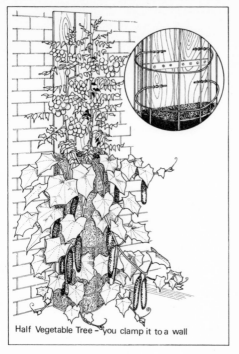

Half Vegetable Tree – you clamp it to a wall

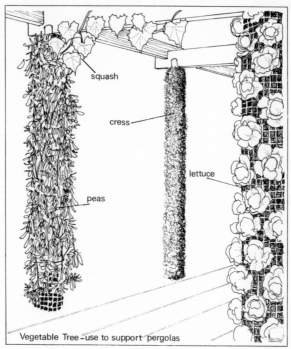

squash

cress

peas

lettuce

Vegetable Tree – use to support pergolas

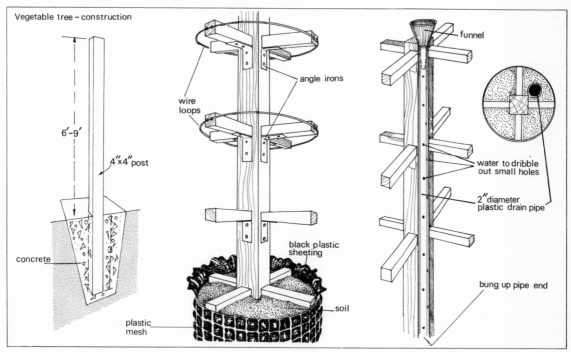

Vegetable tree – construction

6'–9'

4"x4" post

concrete

wire loops

angle irons

black plastic sheeting

plastic mesh

soil

funnel

water to dribble out small holes

2" diameter plastic drain pipe

bung up pipe end

Optimise your garden space by using all the techniques available

mesh. Scatter boxes round the area available. Have a raised bed in the centre. Place three or four tubs against the wall or fence. Fix a shelf or two to the wall for growing vegetables or herbs in pots. Have boxes of different sizes and depths around the raised bed. Vary the colour and texture of your crops from box to box.

For really intensive cropping in confined spaces use frames against all available walls, plus back-to-back frames down the centre of the area if you have room. More about frames, how to make them and how to use them, in the chapter 'Artificial Climates'.

4 Improve Your Soil

Whatever sort of soil you've got, you'll probably wish that you had some other sort. If you live on clay, you'll long for a free-draining sandy soil: if you live on sandy soil, you'll wish you were on loam. If you live on loam count yourself blessed. However, any of these three soil types can very readily be made highly productive.

Raised beds are an expedient you can resort to whatever your soil. However, it limits the space you are likely to use, so it is worth seeing how little you need do to improve what soil you've got.

Clay Soils

These drain badly because the particles are too fine to let water through. In extreme cases, where surface water lies in great puddles, you'll have to lay land drains. How to do this is explained below in the section on hardpan. Normally all you need do is add coarse sand (particle size 0·50 to 1·5 mm) and peat or compost in equal quantities by bulk. Normally if you cover the area you intend to cultivate with a 2–3 in/5–7·5 cm layer, and dig this into the top 9 in/23 cm of soil, mixing soil, sand and compost together thoroughly, you'll have a highly workable soil your first year. If you keep up a regular programme of improvement of this type over 3 or 4 years, you'll find even the most intractable clay soil will turn into a good loam. Once you've got it to the state you want it, keep adding humus, preferably in the form of compost, every year, otherwise the soil will revert to its former clayey state.

Sandy Soils

These need even less work on them than clayey soils. Their main problem is that they drain too fast, which in turn means that all the goodness is washed out of them so that you have drought problems in summer. What they need is the addition of masses of humus: humus, humus and more humus is the recipe here—you just can't add too much. Dig anything from 3–6 in/7·5–15 cm of peat, leaf-mould, compost or manure into the soils each year for 3 years. Then keep digging in lesser quantities every year thereafter. One of the problems of sandy soils is that they usually overlie a sandy substructure, so that the humus you put in just keeps getting washed down to the layers below. That's why you have to keep on adding humus. You want the top 9 in/ 23 cm thick with moisture-retentive humus.

Loam Soils
These are good, workable soils to start with. They generally do not need improving. Just work them carefully, adding a 2 in/5 cm layer of humus each year to replace what you take away from the ground in the way of crops, otherwise they'll deteriorate.

Extreme Soil Types
Consult your county horticultural officer or your state agricultural experimental station.

Subsoils
If you dig down through your soil, you'll usually find that after a while it starts changing colour. The part on the top is called topsoil. The soil underneath, which is usually a different colour or shade, is called subsoil. It has usually lain there, undisturbed, for hundreds of years. So far we have only been discussing topsoil.

All the best books on gardening tell you never to disturb the subsoil, or if you do, to keep it separate from the topsoil. Sound advice. But if you want 8–10 in/20–25 cm of topsoil to grow vegetables and you've only got 4 in/10 cm, what are you to do? Either use raised beds, or add a 4 in/10 cm layer of humus, or humus and sand (depending on your soil type) and dig this into the topsoil, just turning in a couple of inches/ 5 cm of subsoil along with it. Keep doing this year by year and after about 5 years you'll have converted about 10 in/25 cm of subsoil into workable topsoil. The important thing is to bring up only a little subsoil at a time: don't try to convert the whole 10 in/25 cm into top soil in one season. Can't be done. No way.

Hardpan
This is the most dreaded of all subsoils. It is as hard as a metalled highway surface and just about as impervious. Water simply will not drain through it. If the water won't drain, the plants will drown. So somehow you've got to drain it.

Here's what you do. Decide which end of your garden you are going to have the compost bin, tool shed, bonfire patch, and somewhere down that end, dig right through the hardpan. You'll know when you're through: the digging suddenly becomes easier. The hole should be 3–4 ft/1–1·2 m in diameter—even in a small garden—and may need to be 6 or 8 ft/2–2·4 m deep. It's hard work, but if you've got hardpan problems you've got to do it, or you'll never grow anything. Incidentally, once you get down into that hole you'll find you haven't got room to wield a pick. So take the haft out of the pick, and wedge one of the pick

Corn silhouetted against a summer sky

Purple sprouting broccoli

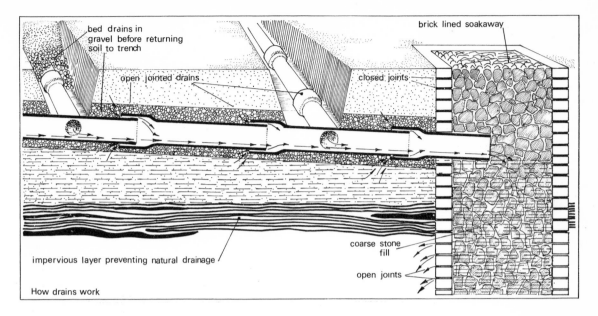

bed drains in gravel before returning soil to trench

open jointed drains

closed joints

brick lined soakaway

impervious layer preventing natural drainage

coarse stone fill

open joints

How drains work

blades into a scaffolding bar. Then thrust the pick down into the hole, pulling the scaffolding pole against the edge of the hole to lever the soil loose.

Once, you've dug your hole, fill it with broken bricks, old rocks and the like. Then lay land drains in a herring-bone pattern, the spine of the herring-bone emptying into the soakaway you've just dug. Make sure the drains have a fall of between 1 in 40–1 in 60, use clay or composition pipes, packed round with coarse pebbles. The shallowest of the drains should be at least 8 in/20 cm under the soil surface. If you lay these drains properly, they should last anything from 10 to 20 years.

Getting the pH Right

Vegetables grow best when the pH is neutral or slightly on the alkaline side of neutral, roughly pH 6 and pH 7. You may just be lucky enough to have the right pH to start with, but even if you have, read on, because as you add fertilisers you will gradually change the pH. Peat will make soil more acid—lime more alkaline. Test or have tested the pH of your soil at least once every 5 years. Once it moves out of the pH 6 to 7 area you need to take corrective action.

To correct an acid soil (pH 6 or below), add lime. The problem is always to know at what rate to apply it. This will vary considerably on the type of soil you live on. For example, if you live on a quick draining sandy soil it will take you about 30 lbs/14 kg of lime per 1,000 sq ft/ 93 m² to raise the pH from 4·5 to 5·5. If you live on good loam it will take about 60 lbs/28 kg to raise the pH by the same amount over the same area. If you live on heavy clay it will take about 90 lbs/42 kg to

Scarlet runner beans form rampant vines as attractive for their flowers as their harvest

achieve the same result. If you're in doubt as to what rate to apply the lime, seek expert advice from your county horticultural officer or state agricultural experimental station. Don't take the word of your local garden centre; they always want to sell you more than you need anyway.

There are several types of lime available. The most commonly used is slaked or burnt lime. The best is ground Dolomitic limestone, which lasts longer in the ground and has the advantage of containing magnesium: many soils are mildly deficient in magnesium.

To make an alkaline soil more acid keep digging in moss peat. It is impossible to give accurate rates of application since the pH of the peat varies, so test the soil yearly till you get the pH right.

All this may sound very scientific and precise. So it is. But gardening is an art, not an exact science. The facts and figures here are for the scientifically-minded perfectionist. Vegetables are tolerant of widely varying soils. Try to get your soil as neutral as you can, but don't worry about the odd decimal point on the pH scale. Alternatively, try everything, and then concentrate on what you find does well in your soil.

Changing Your Soil pH in Relation to Your Soil Type

pH	SOIL ACIDITY	LIGHT SANDY SOILS	SANDY LOAM OR SILT SOILS	MEDIUM LOAM SOILS	CLAY LOAM SOILS	HEAVY CLAY SOILS
6·0	Moderate	2 lbs	3 lbs	4 lbs	5 lbs	$5\frac{1}{2}$–6 lbs
5·5	Strong	3 lbs	4 lbs	$5\frac{3}{4}$ lbs	7 lbs	$7\frac{3}{4}$ lbs
5·0	Very strong	$3\frac{3}{4}$ lbs	$5\frac{3}{4}$ lbs	$7\frac{1}{4}$ lbs	8 lbs	$9\frac{1}{4}$ lbs
4·5	Extreme	4 lbs	$6\frac{1}{2}$ lbs	8 lbs	$8\frac{3}{4}$ lbs	10 lbs

Amount of hydrated lime required to raise pH 6·5, the optimum level. Rate per 100 sq ft.

5 What Plants Eat

People eat plants. But what do plants eat?

Plants take the energy from sunlight and use it to convert simple inorganic substances into highly complex organic compounds which men and animals can eat.

The most important of these plant foods are, perhaps surprisingly, hydrogen, oxygen and carbon. Plants obtain these from the air and water available to their roots in the soil. Which is one good reason why a really good soil structure matters. You can't actually supply the plants with neat hydrogen, oxygen and carbon, as you can most of their other foods: the most you can do is make sure your soil has the best structure you can give it.

Beyond that there are a number of minerals which the plants derive from the soil and absorb through their roots in the form of weak salt solutions. There are dozens of minerals which plants draw on, but three are much more important than the others. These three are known as the macro-elements. The others are the micro-elements.

The important three are nitrogen, phosphorus and potassium. All plants draw heavily on these three. Nitrogen in particular. Apply soluble nitrogen to the growing mix round a plant and you will see its growth accelerate literally over night. Potassium is used for flowering and fruit-setting. Phosphorus helps plants grow the right colour.

Calcium is almost as important. It occurs naturally in most soils. Plants use it to build their cell walls. It's the calcium in the cell walls that makes lettuce crisp for example. Provided your soil pH is right you should have no calcium problems. In acid soils the calcium is usually present but the plants can't use it. Lime releases it.

The micro-elements are used by plants in tiny quantities, and thus are sometimes known as trace elements. They consist of all sorts of rare metals and minerals, like caesium, boron, platinum—even gold. By and large there is quite enough of these elements in the soil for the plants, and they are unlikely to run out of them. However, there are two that are sometimes in short supply in soils: these are magnesium and boron. These deficiencies usually occur in sandy, fast-draining soils.

6 Feeding Your Plants

Now you know what plants eat. The only problem is how to feed them.

There are two ways you can feed them. You can either give them artificial fertilizers, or you can give them organic manure. Each has its advantage and its disadvantage. The great plus for artificial fertilizers is that you know exactly what proportions of which plant foods you are giving them. The disadvantage is that you are not building humus. The great plus for organic manures is that you are building humus. The disadvantage is that you do not know exactly what proportions of which plant foods you are giving them. Since humus building is as important as feeding the plants, the sensible thing is to use both artificial fertilizers and organic manures.

There's another good reason for using both. Artificial fertilizers release their food as soon as they combine with the moisture in the soil. Organic manures release their foods slowly. For example: you can give plants nitrogen in the form of sodium nitrate. It's a chemical. It produces instant food for the plants. Or you can give it in the form of dried slaughterhouse products. Which is organic. It will release its nitrogen slowly as it decays under the action of soil micro-organisms. So, apart from building humus, organic manures do have the advantage that they supply plants with food over a far longer period than artificial fertilizers.

By using both, you gain both ways.

The prime foods of all plants are nitrogen, phosphorus and potassium. These are known respectively by their symbols as N, P and K. (N = nitrogen, P = phosphorus, K = potassium.) All 'complete' fertilizers contain all three, and by law, the packets have to state the percentages of each. They are always stated in the same order— N, P, K. Thus 10–10–10 is 10% N to 10% P to 10% K. 6–12–18 is 6% N to 12% P to 18% K. Artificial fertilizers are available in differing proportions of these main elements. Different crops demand different fertilizers.

Increasingly, especially in America, manufacturers have been adding trace elements, mainly boron and magnesium, in minute quantities, to 'complete' fertilizers. This is on the 'play safe' principle. Since plants won't use these elements unless they need them, there's no harm in adding them. It's just a waste of money.

Recently manufacturers have started increasing the concentration of the ingredients in fertilizers. The ratios remain the same, but you need less fertilizer for the same area. Watch the packages: don't get caught out.

Always read manufacturer's instructions. Apply exactly according to the instructions. There is no point in using more fertilizer than the plants can use. The excess does not simply stay in the soil for next year. It gets leached away by the action of rain.

It's all very well to talk of using both artificial fertilizers and organic manures, but organic manures are becoming increasingly hard to obtain. Up to a point that's understandable. The more urbanised we become the further the fields and farms move away. None the less, if animals eat they've got to excrete: and animals do eat. So there are natural manures around. The NPK chart shows the relative amounts of N, P and K available in some of the organic manures most commonly available. The figures are obviously not as precise as for artificial fertilizers made to rigidly controlled standards. You can't control what goes into organic manure that precisely.

Approximate N, P, K, content of some commonly available organic manures and mulches.

MATERIAL	%N	%P	%K
Bat guano	10·0	4·0	2·0
Blood & Bone	6·5	7·0	—
Bone Meal	3·0	15·0	—
Good Garden Compost	1·5	2·0	0·7
Cow Manure	0·6	0·4	0·3
Dried Blood	13·0	2·0	1·0
Farmyard Manure	0·6	0·4	0·5
Fish Meal	10·0	4·0	—
Hoof & Horn	12·0	2·0	—
Horse Manure	0·7	0·5	0·6
Pig Manure	0·5	0·3	0·4
Poultry Manure	1·6	1·8	7·0
Sewer Sludge	0·5	0·5	0·2
Town Waste	1·2	0·5	0·3
Sedge Peat	1·0	1·5	0·6
Sphagnum Peat	0·5	1·0	0·3
Spent Hops	0·4	1·2	2·0
Seaweed	0·3	1·3	2·3

Composting

With organic manures becoming harder and harder to obtain, more and more people are turning to composting. The purpose of composting is to turn normal garden and organic household waste into a rich, brown, spongy substance that looks and smells very like top grade moss peat. It is a first-rate source of humus, and when well made contains most of the foods plants need in relatively high quantities. In fact it's one of the finest organic manures you can get.

Here's how you make it.

First of all decide where you want your compost bin. It needs to be near your vegetable patch so that you don't have to carry or wheel the compost far in order to put in on the vegetable patch. On the other hand, put it somewhere where it is easily reached from the house, since you'll want household waste going on it too. Ideally you need three bins: one full and ready for use; one filled and composting; one being filled.

If you've ever heard of compost heaps, forget them: they are untidy and inefficient at composting. Start thinking of compost bins. They're tidy, and they compost every shred of material you put into them. Either buy or build three bins. Important points to look for are these: the bin should have the bottom raised off the ground so that air can circulate under the heap: there should be holes in the sides, so that air

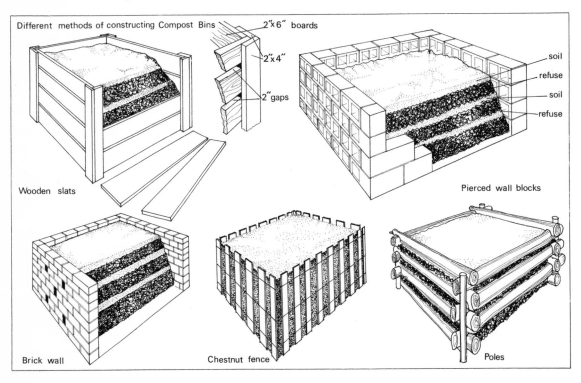

Different methods of constructing Compost Bins

2″x 6″ boards
2″x 4″
2″ gaps

soil
refuse
soil
refuse

Wooden slats

Pierced wall blocks

Brick wall

Chestnut fence

Poles

can get in there too. Given those prerequisites, you can build a bin from wooden slats, poles, chestnut fencing, wire or extruded plastic netting, bricks, concrete blocks or even pierced wall blocks.

Then start filling your first bin. Put in waste matter from the garden: lawn clippings, green weeds, dry weeds, yellowing leaves from ripening vegetables and generally any garden waste. Once you realise the true value of compost start adding vegetable refuse from the kitchen: vegetable peelings, and any parts of vegetables you don't eat. Eggshells provide a valuable source of calcium. Enthusiasts add all sorts of other waste: emptyings from the vacuum cleaner, shredded newspapers, paper bags, cardboard boxes and so on.

Generally woody materials take far longer to rot than green waste. Twigs from hedge clippings take about 8 times as long as soft green waste. If you have a shredder, shred clippings like these into small lengths: they'll compost in half the time that way. Otherwise put them on the bonfire: they're just as useful burned. Bonfire ash is a prime home source of potash or potassium, which helps vegetables grow a good colour.

Once you've got an even layer about 6–8 in/15–20 cm deep, close it off with a 2 in/5 cm layer of garden soil, manure, peat, leaf-mould or some similar non-green substance. You can add an activator at this stage. Many brands are available. Use according to the maker's instructions. Or use organic manure or an artificial fertilizer. The purpose is to help feed the bacteria in the heap which break down the green material into that rich brown compost you want at the end of your efforts. Keep building the cake up in layers till you reach the top of the bin. Keep the heap always damp, never wet. In high rainfall areas keep the bin covered. Keep it covered all winter too. Just use black plastic sheeting weighted down with bricks or rocks. Aim for the consistency of a squeezed out sponge.

Once you reach the top of the bin, level off with a layer of earth or peat. Then leave for two weeks.

During this period the compost in the bin should heat up to about 150°F/65°C, which is hot enough to kill off all weed seeds and pests and diseases. If the heap gets too hot the contents will become a sludgy mess: if it does not become hot enough weed seeds won't be killed. Some people even take the temperature of their compost heaps: you've really got to believe in compost as an end in itself to bother to do that. You'll get good enough compost if you just follow these instructions.

You'll know when the compost is ready to use in two ways. The temperature will drop: that's your first clue. Then it will start smelling fresh and earthy. Check that it is ready to use by feel: when ready it will be dark brown in colour and should crumble between your fingers.

7 Water and Watering

Water is crucial to everything that lives. Plants in particular. Compare a rainfall map of your country with a vegetation map of your country, and you'll see at once that the richest and most varied flora occurs where the rainfall is high but not excessive. True, plants can live in deserts, but they've had to make special adaptations to survive there. Vegetables can't: most of them come from the cool temperate regions of the world, or mountainous regions, with a rainfall of between 30 and 50/75 cm and 1·2 m a year.

There are two reasons why plants need water. The first is that they can only absorb plant foods in the form of weak solutions. Put all the fertilizer in the world round a plant, but if you don't wet it, it's useless to the plant.

The other is that a very high proportion of a plant is water. A cauliflower, for example, is 96% water; a ripe tomato is 94% water; a ripe watermelon, 93%; cabbages are 92% and broccoli 89%. All of which may surprise you. It shouldn't because you, like every other human, fat or thin, are 70% water yourself. Much of your water content got there because you eat vegetables. And the vegetables got their water content from the soil.

Vegetables absorb water from the soil in much the same way as dry blotting-paper soaks up water from a cup. However, that only works so long as there is moisture in the soil. If the soil dries out the process is reversed, and the soil starts absorbing water from the plants. When this happens you have drought. And dead vegetables. At the other extreme, too much water in the soil, and the vegetables drown—literally: they need water and air in the soil in roughly equal proportions. If all the air passages in the soil are full of water, roots die off. Then rot sets in. Then you have more dead vegetables. It really sounds as though you can't win either way. But you can.

What most vegetables need is an even supply of water, never too much, never too little. Just how much water to give and how often to give it depends entirely on your soil. You need to water more often on a sandy, quick-draining soil than you do on a heavy, moisture-retaining clay soil.

Hand Testing Method of Deciding When to Water

AMOUNT OF AVAILABLE SOIL MOISTURE	FINE TEXTURE e.g. CLAYS	MEDIUM TEXTURE e.g. SANDY LOAM	COARSE TEXTURE e.g. SANDY SOILS
None	Cracked surface, hard baked appearance	Small lumps breaking down into powder	Loose falling through fingers
Less than half	Lumps form easily	Crumb-like, but can form lump if squeezed	Looks dry and will not form any lumps if handled
Half–Three-quarters	'Fingers' of soil formed when rubbed between hands	Pliable lump forms which smears when rubbed between finger and thumb	Crumbling formed lump
Over Three-quarters	Sticky mess. Very pliable and can be modelled into rings	Very pliable lump formed which sticks to hands	Crumbling lump formed which disintegrates with pressure

Apply water at half-way line

Experienced gardeners get to know their plants, and know when to water by reading almost intuitively tiny little telltale signs on the plants. First-time gardeners might do well to invest in a moisture meter. This tells you simply, on a graduated scale, whether the soil is dry, moist or wet. It ought to be in the moist area. Use the meter, which consists of a head which gives you the reading, and a spike, by pushing the spike into the soil. The tip of the spike is made from a different metal from the rest of the spike. Any moisture in the soil sets up an electrolytic reaction which moves the needle on the dial. No moisture and you get a dry reading. Too much water and you get a wet reading. Wait till the meter is on the low side of moist coming on to dry, then give the plants a soaking. A good soaking once a week does the plants far more good than a light overhead sprinkle once a day. Water applied like that encourages roots to grow upwards, and then scorch in the sun.

Always keep the moisture meter clean. Never leave soil on the spike: it corrodes it. Clean the spike either with a dry rag or wash it in distilled water. One odd thing you may notice: if you dip the spike in distilled water you will get a dry reading. You need mineral salts in the water to get any reading at all. Add salt or detergent and the reading will shoot up to wet.

How to Apply Water

The traditional, time-honoured way of watering vegetables is with a watering can. It certainly delivers a concentrated dose of water in the right place. It does one or two other things too: like compacting the soil, or washing it away from the roots of the vegetable. If you must water with a watering can, and it's fine for some plants like melons and squashes, set a flowerpot in the ground beside the plant, and pour the water into that.

Far more effective are oscillating sprayers fitted to the end of a hose. These swing back and forth delivering a quite convincing imitation of rain, giving good penetration of the soil. Even more effective, are tall stands which deliver a mist-like spray. This very fine spray is even more penetrating than that delivered by an oscillating sprayer.

Never use any sort of overhead watering device—one that wets the leaves of plants as well as the soil—during strong sunlight. Use it only early morning or early evening. Droplets of water resting on leaves, flowers and fruit concentrate the sun's rays and can cause scorching of the leaves or fruit.

Depth of Rooting in Vegetables

When to water can be critical. This is not determined by whether the top inch or two of soil seems dry, but by whether the soil is dry at the depth at which the growing roots are feeding. The following gives some guidance as to the depths to which various vegetables push their roots into soil, assuming an unlimited depth of fertile topsoil. In fact, most vegetables will grow well in raised beds of good soil no more than 8 to 12 inches deep.

SHALLOW ROOTING TO 18 INCHES DEEP	MODERATELY DEEP TO 36 INCHES DEEP	DEEP ROOTING TO 48 INCHES DEEP
Broccoli	Beans (push and pole)	Artichoke
Brussels sprouts	Chard	Asparagus
Cabbage	Cucumber	Beans (Lima)
Cauliflower	Eggplant	Leek
Celery	Muskmelon	Onion
Chinese cabbage	Peas	Pumpkin
Corn	Pepper	Sweet potato
Endive	Rutabaga	Tomato
Lettuce	Summer squash	Watermelon
Potato	Turnip	Winter squash
Radish		
Spinach		

Watering Frequencies

The frequency with which you need to water crops depends upon the depth to which their roots penetrate, since that is where the water is needed, and the type of soil you have. The chart below shows what the intervals would be assuming that the soil's potential moisture retention was 50% depleted. It also assumes that there has been no rainfall, and none is expected. To use the chart, find the vegetable you want to water on the chart showing root depths, then follow the depth line across the chart till you come to the diagonal line showing your type of soil: then move upwards to the days between watering line. For example: lettuce, a shallow rooting crop, maximum depth 18 inches. However, you're growing it in raised beds, so assume a root depth of 12 inches. Find the 12 inch line on the left hand side of the chart and follow it across until you come to the diagonal showing loam. Move upwards to the watering frequency line. You need to water lettuce every 5 to 6 days. On sandy soil you would need to water it every 2 to 3 days: on clay soils every 8 or 9 days. If nothing else, the chart tells you that the shallower the roots of the crop, the more frequently you need to water, the deeper the roots the less often.

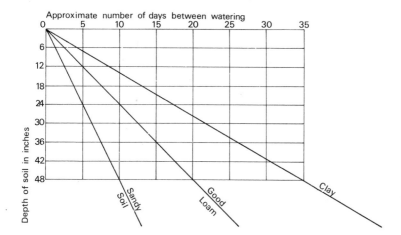

An alternative to sprinklers, and one well worth considering since it is time-saving, is the use of a perforated hose. This is simply a hose with very small holes punctured all along its length. You can buy a single perforated hose, but more effective are double or triple welded hoses. These are simply plastic hoses welded together: they give far better water distribution. The spray is fine and even a mild breeze blows the spray about enough to prevent puddling where the jets fall.

Irrigation Ditches

These are almost essential in arid areas. If you intend to use them, place the rows of vegetables twice as far apart as recommended. Dig a ditch 9–12 in/23–30 cm wide and 6 in/15 cm deep between each row. Link all the ditches into a transverse feeder ditch at one or other end of the rows. Feed the water from a broad bore hose into the feeder ditch. To stop the

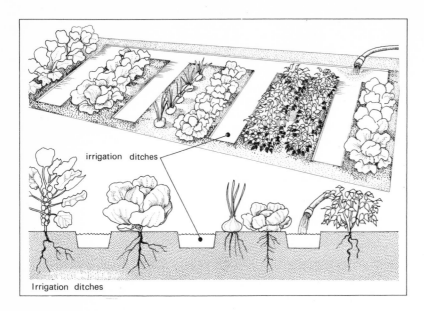

irrigation ditches

Irrigation ditches

water washing soil away as it comes out of the hose, tie a stocking round it, or a piece of old burlap. If you want to block off any particular channel just put a piece of board across where it meets the feeder ditch.

You'll usually find you trample the ground at the bottom of the ditches hard enough to ensure good water distribution anyway, but you get even better distribution of water if you line the ditches. There are lots of ways you can do this. The simplest, and it usually only lasts a single season, is simply to lay heavy duty plastic sheeting along the bottom of the ditches. A more sophisticated method is to line the ditches with plastic sheeting, taking it up the sides as well as along the base. Leave the plastic sheeting in the feeder channel intact, but puncture leakage holes in the sides of the lesser irrigation ditches. After all, it's the water that goes out of the sides of the ditches that does the vegetables most good. What drains out of the bottom of the ditches is largely wasted.

For permanent channels lay paving slabs along the bottom of the channels, fitting them as tightly as you can. Then lay slabs along the sides of the lesser ditches; lay them at 45°, and make sure that they do not fit too well: the water must be able to seep through the gaps between the slabs on the sides. The best plan of all is to use slabs on the sides that are half the size of the slabs on the bottom. That increases your sideways leakage fourfold.

8 Climate

People who play games talk about weather. People who grow plants talk about climate. There is a difference. Weather is a temporary, passing trivial phenomenon, like whether it is going to rain on your barbecue night, or how cold it was yesterday. Climate is a fixed asset (or liability, according to where you live) based on the accurate measurement of passing phenomena like rain, frost and sun, and the patterns in which they are combined in different parts of the world.

Phenomena like precipitation (which embraces rainfall, snow and mist), number of days of clear sun, dates of first and last frost, degree of freezing, number of frost free days, minimum winter temperature and maximum summer temperature are the sort of things that are measured. In America, over 2,000 weather stations have kept records of this type for over 35 years. In Britain, some 300 stations have kept records, in some cases for nearly 80 years. As a result of all this record keeping, some fairly accurate information is available about climate in various parts of both America and Britain.

In America, good use of this information has been made, converting it into climatic zones, each of which has known characteristics. No one has bothered to do this for Britain. It's such a tiny place it's hardly worth doing. You could fit Great Britain into Texas eight times. Scale matters. One US climatic zone embraces the whole of Britain. Texas, by contrast, sprawls across sections of six zones.

Most American readers will already be familiar with climatic zone maps. However, for the benefit of British readers and first-time American gardeners, here's how they work. The US Department of Agriculture and the Arnold Arboretum, America's equivalent of Kew, have each independently divided America up into a number of zones based primarily on minimum winter temperatures. Happily the two have arrived at similar zone patterns. The important thing to remember when using US zone maps is that the lower the zone number, the colder the winter, the higher the number the hotter.

From all of which it would seem that, if you live in Britain and you want to work out to which US climatic zone your neck of the woods corresponds, all you have to do is find your average winter temperature,

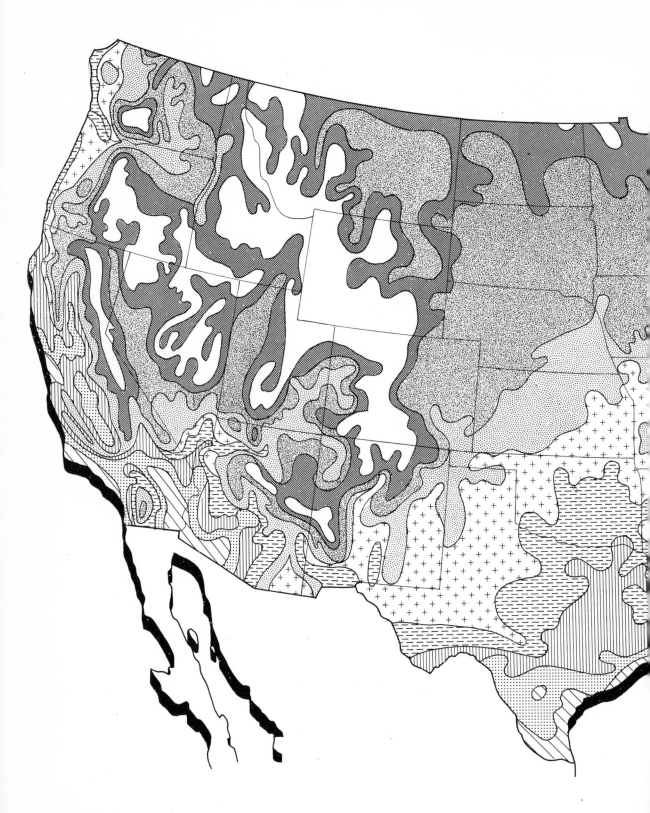

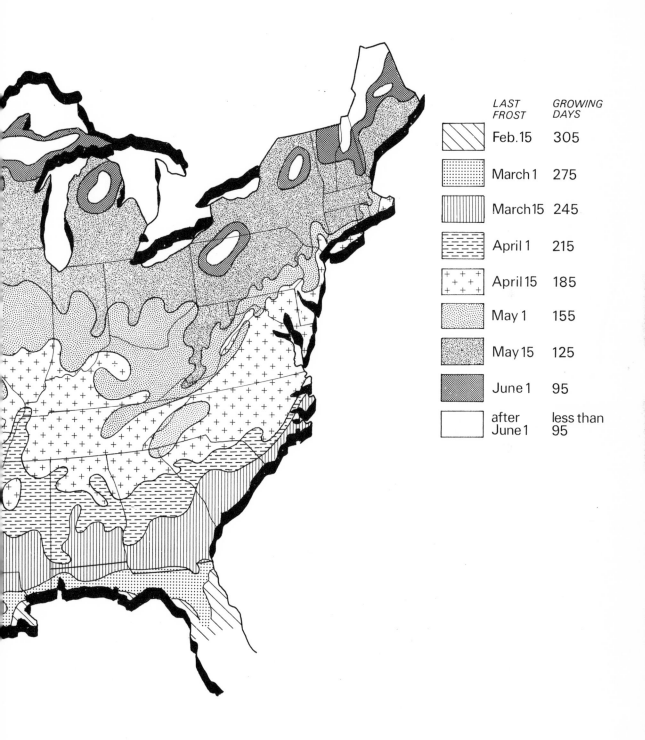

	LAST FROST	GROWING DAYS
	Feb.15	305
	March 1	275
	March 15	245
	April 1	215
	April 15	185
	May 1	155
	May 15	125
	June 1	95
	after June 1	less than 95

and see which zone that marries with. Take an example. The average minimum winter temperature in London is 32°F/0°C. In which case it corresponds to US climatic zone 9. Just one problem. US climatic zone 9 is rated sub-tropical—which is hardly a fitting description of a grey wet midsummer's day in London. If one looks instead at maximum summer temperatures, then London, with a summer maximum of about 64°F/18°C, would belong in zone 3, which means it ought to have a winter minimum of −35°F/−20°C—which it doesn't. Correspondences are not that easy. One has to remember that America has a continental climate; Britain a maritime climate. In America winters are on average longer and harder than in Britain, summers shorter but hotter and sunnier. If you must have a direct correspondence, London ⌒ Seattle, as near as may be.

However, so far as vegetables are concerned, direct correspondences of this type are not particularly important. Vegetables are the most tolerant of all plants cultivated by man. The longer a plant is in cultivation, the more adaptable it becomes to soil, climate, winter cold and summer heat. And man encourages this, forever breeding more cold-tolerant varieties of this or that, or more heat-tolerant varieties of something else. The common cabbage, for example, a native of the chalk-lands of the Mediterranean basin, can be grown in America from mid Saskatchewan in zone 2, where winter temperatures can drop to −50°F/−40°C to the southern tip of Texas in zone 10 where the coldest they've ever had it is about 30°F/−1·1°C, and summer temperatures shoot up into the upper 80s F/over 30°C.

Because of this tolerance of temperature variations, Britain and America can be divided quite simply into three zones for the purpose of vegetable growing. These are the Hardy zone, the Half-hardy zone and the Tender zone. All the vegetables listed in this book are rated as Hardy, Half-hardy or Tender. Each is hardy in its own zone. Thus a vegetable labelled Hardy is hardy in the Hardy zone but needs to be started under glass in the Half-hardy zone. In the Tender zone, grow it in winter instead of summer. A Half-hardy vegetable is hardy in the Half-hardy zone and the Tender zone, but needs to be started in frames or a greenhouse in the Hardy zone. Vegetables labelled Tender are hardy in the Tender zone but need to be started under glass in the Half-hardy zone and grown entirely under glass in the Hardy zone.

There are two other climatic factors you need to understand if you are to grow vegetables successfully. These are last frost dates, and number of growing days: the two are closely interrelated. The number of growing days you have is a vital unit of information. So you need to know what growing days are. They are the number of days that elapse between your last and your first frost. If your last frost is on 1 June and your first frost on 15 August, then your number of growing days is 76. So if you want to grow, for example, a pumpkin, which needs 120 growing days to mature, you can't do it. At least you can't do it out of doors.

Tomatoes are probably the most colourful and rewarding of all the crops you can grow

Young peas developing in their pods

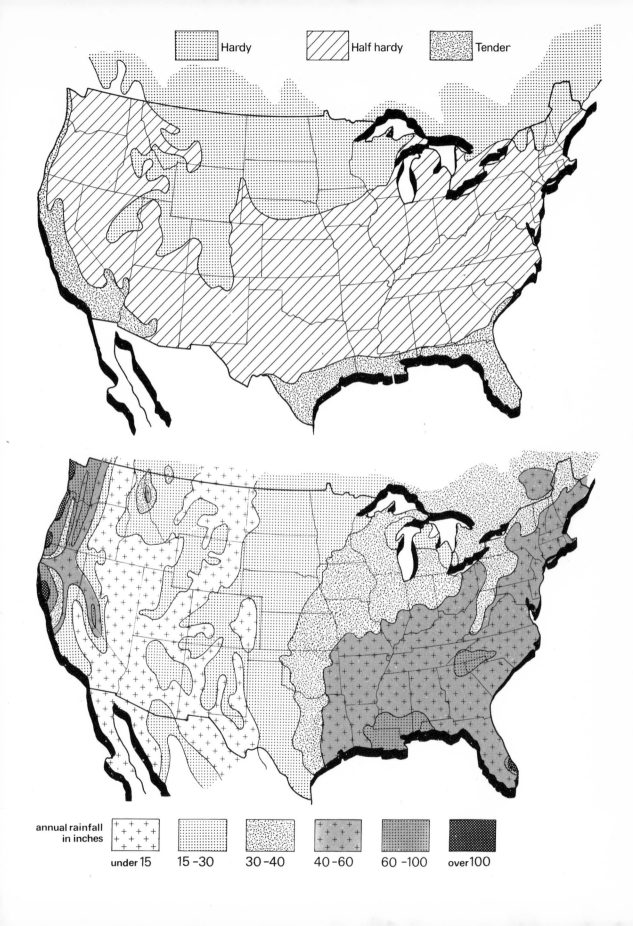

Hardy   Half hardy   Tender

annual rainfall
in inches

under 15   15 -30   30 -40   40 -60   60 -100   over 100

If your number of growing days is insufficient for the plant you want to grow, you'll have to start it under glass, unless the vegetable is hardy in your area. The relationship between last frost and number of growing days is obvious: the later your last frost, the earlier your first frost, so the fewer the number of growing days available to you.

Maps in this book show you the three hardiness zones. Other maps show you the dates of your last killing frost. A killing frost is $32°F/0°C$. The maps give you the number of growing days at various key points in Britain and America. Look up where you live on the map, locate the nearest station for which growing days are given, and this will give you a pretty good idea of what to expect and what you can grow.

When you come to Part Two of this book, you'll find that for nearly all the vegetables there will be an instruction such as 'plant out two weeks after the last killing frost'. That's why you need to know when your last killing frost should occur. There is a 50% probability that it will actually occur on the day it is supposed to. Gambler gardeners sometimes think they can beat the seasons: plant a little earlier, or a little later. Sometimes they're lucky: but one snap frost and they've lost the crop. If you're a first-time gardener, stick to the rules. Start breaking them as you gain confidence.

If you're not content with the climate you live in, or you find you can't improve the microclimate sufficiently for your needs, there's one more option open to you. Create your own artificial climate. That's what the next chapter is about.

Influence of slope of ground on growing season. Soil warms quickest when the sun's rays strike it at right angles. South-facing slopes warm quicker than zone average, north-facing slopes more slowly than zone average, level land at zone average time.

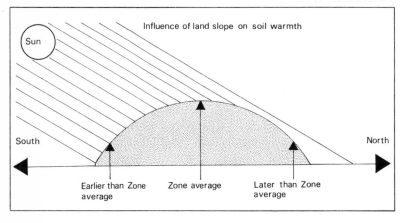

9 Artificial Climates

If you live in an adverse climate and want to extend your growing season or double your rate of vegetable production, the answer is to create your own entirely artificial miniclimate. You can do this by erecting a greenhouse, or more simply by using frames. Devices like these are especially useful for small-space gardeners.

Frames

While Americans are busy rediscovering the virtues of old-fashioned frames, the British are busy forgetting about frames and putting up greenhouses—roughly 60% of British garden owners have a greenhouse. Each could learn from the other, especially in vegetable growing, and especially as the British use their greenhouses mainly for ornamental plants.

The simplest type of frame consists of four pieces of wood, a low front board, a tall back board and two sides sloping downwards towards the front. On top of this is placed a large window, hinged to the high back of the lower section. For some reason the glass part of a frame is called a 'light'. The light may either be hinged to the back of the frame, in which case it is a permanent fixture, or it can be hooked to the back, so that it can be removed altogether in high summer. The light is opened from the front, and is so arranged that it can be propped open

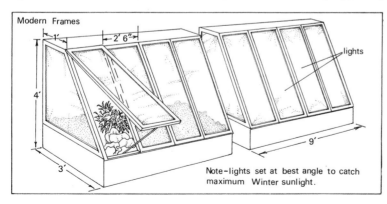

Modern Frames

1' 2' 6" lights

4'

3'

9'

Note—lights set at best angle to catch maximum Winter sunlight.

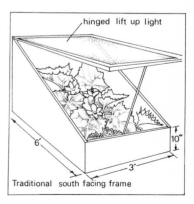

hinged lift up light

Traditional south facing frame

6' 3' 10"

varying amounts, a little at first to harden young seedlings, then more, then even more once the plants are in full growth. Traditionally such frames are so designed that the plants are grown in the ground. Ideally the slope of the light should face south, to trap maximum sunlight and warmth. You can make a frame like this yourself, building the sides from wood, brick or concrete blocks. Build the frame to take a standard-size window. Or pick up a second-hand window, then build the frame to fit it. You can glaze the light either with glass or clear plastic sheeting: the disadvantage of plastic is that you get more condensation inside it, and it needs replacing every couple of years since it becomes brittle owing to a chemical reaction set up by ultra-violet.

A frame like that will give you a couple of weeks' start on your neighbours. Use it to sow seed, grow on seedlings and then harden them off before planting out. In midsummer plant a crop to ripen after first frosts: use the lights to keep high day temperatures inside the frame.

You can get even more benefit from your frames if you improve on this traditional model. The first step is to raise the soil level, so that in effect you have a frame on a raised bed. You already know that a raised bed can give you a fortnight's start on your neighbours, so a raised bed/ frame combination should give you nearly a month's headway on them.

Next, improve the light and heat-catching properties of your frame. The traditional design does not optimise the available sun's light or heat: the glass is at the wrong angle. To get maximum sunlight penetration, the glass should be at right angles to the sun's rays. If the sun hits the glass at $90°$, 90% of the sun's light will penetrate the glass. If it hits the glass at $80°$ 80% will penetrate: at $70°$, 70% will penetrate and so on. At $30°$ only 30% will penetrate. The rest just bounces off due to the refractive properties of glass. On a traditional frame the glass is set at an angle of about $20°$. That means that in midwinter in Philadelphia, for example, the sun's rays are hitting the glass at an angle of $6\frac{1}{2}°$, so that only about $24\frac{1}{2}\%$ of the available sunlight is getting into the frame. If the glass were set at $63\frac{1}{2}°$ instead, 90% of the light would get into the frame. That's how much difference getting the frame angle right can mean. Frames too, should always be aligned due east/west.

Just one problem. If you live on the equator the sun is straight overhead—all year round. The further away from the equator you move, the greater the angle at which the sun reaches you. Since you want the sun's rays to strike the lights at an angle of $90°$, you'll need the light horizontal at the equator, but you'll need to move it nearer and nearer to the vertical the further you move from the equator.

There's just one more hitch you have to think of. The sun at noon at the summer solstice is much higher in the sky than it is at noon at the winter solstice. Again, the difference between the angle of incidence in summer and winter becomes greater the further you move away from the Equator—a mere $37°$ difference at latitude 30, $47°$ difference at latitude 60. The ideal frame would obviously be designed with each light made of three panes set at different angles: the most vertical to catch the winter sun, the nearest to horizontal to catch summer sun, and the third to catch spring and autumn sun.

Fortunately there's no need to complicate things so much for frames. By and large you'll get enough light and warmth in the frame in summer anyway. So set the light to catch maximum winter sun: so that the sun's rays strike the glass at right angles at the winter solstice at your latitude. 90% of the sun's rays that hit the glass at 90° will penetrate the glass.

Angle of incidence of the sun's rays and ideal glass angles for frames at different latitudes.

LATITUDE	ANGLE AT SUMMER SOLSTICE	ANGLE AT WINTER SOLSTICE	IDEAL GLASS ANGLE FOR WINTER LIGHT
30	$83\frac{1}{2}°$	$36\frac{1}{2}°$	$53\frac{1}{2}°$
35	$78\frac{1}{2}°$	$31\frac{1}{2}°$	$58\frac{1}{2}°$
40	$73\frac{1}{2}°$	$26\frac{1}{2}°$	$63\frac{1}{2}°$
45	$68\frac{1}{2}°$	$21\frac{1}{2}°$	$68\frac{1}{2}°$
50	$63\frac{1}{2}°$	$16\frac{1}{2}°$	$73\frac{1}{2}°$
55	$58\frac{1}{2}°$	$11\frac{1}{2}°$	$78\frac{1}{2}°$
60	$53\frac{1}{2}°$	$6\frac{1}{2}°$	$83\frac{1}{2}°$

*The angle given as ideal for the glass in the light is given in degrees from level ground.

**For perfectionists the equation is: 90° -- angle of incidence of sun's rays = angle of glass from ground. The angle of incidence and the angle of the glass always add up to 90°. Worked example: Latitude $47\frac{1}{2}$. Angle of incidence 19°. $90 - 19 = 71$. 71° would therefore be the ideal angle for the glass in the frame.

A quick glance at the diagram showing the correct angle of the glass in frames shows at once that the glass should be far nearer the vertical than it is in old-fashioned frames. This has two great advantages over conventional frames, apart, of course, from catching more light. In the first place it means that frost (which is heavy and sinks) will tend to fall rapidly away from the steeply facing glass, and secondly, it means that much taller crops can be grown in the frames or, alternatively, that several layers of vegetables can be grown at the same time. Loss of depth can easily be countered by having a nearly horizontal light at the top of the frame. This should be double-glazed because frost will tend to settle there.

The ideal angle for the glass on frames in southern Britain would be about 70°. In Scotland north of Edinburgh it would be about 80°. For American equivalent angles, see **Angle of Incidence Chart**.

All of which is pie-in-the-sky utopia-talk because you'll probably

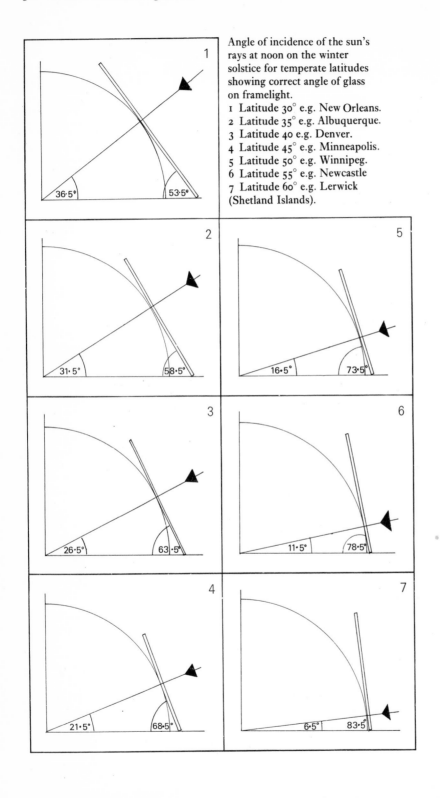

Angle of incidence of the sun's rays at noon on the winter solstice for temperate latitudes showing correct angle of glass on framelight.

1 Latitude 30° e.g. New Orleans.
2 Latitude 35° e.g. Albuquerque.
3 Latitude 40 e.g. Denver.
4 Latitude 45° e.g. Minneapolis.
5 Latitude 50° e.g. Winnipeg.
6 Latitude 55° e.g. Newcastle
7 Latitude 60° e.g. Lerwick
(Shetland Islands).

Timber Laths - protect vegetables from strong sunlight.

Blankets, Rugs or Coconut matting to conserve heat on cold frosty nights.

Glass or Rigid Plastic – double glazing to protect vegetables from snow and too much rain.

Fine Plastic or Wire mesh screen –keeps out leaves, birds, in– –sect pests and filters winds.

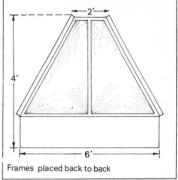

Frames placed back to back

find that the only place in your backyard where you can line up the frame due east-west prevents you getting into the back door and is in shade for most of the day anyway. Faced with this sort of situation, just place the frame wherever it will get most sunlight falling on it.

If you want to use the frame as a veritable vegetable factory for year round production, you'll need to heat it. Use coaxial soil-warming cables buried in a layer of grit below the growing mix. Control soil temperature with a thermostat linked to a thermometer set in the soil. Heat the air with coaxial cables all round the inside of the frame. Control air temperature with a different thermostat, linked to a rod-type thermometer set in the air space inside the frame.

Use a framework of laths running vertically across the light to shade vegetables from too strong sunlight. Use a rug, blanket or coconut matting to conserve heat on icy winter nights. Use an additional light of glass or rigid plastic sheeting to provide double glazing to conserve heat in frames during daylight in winter, or to provide extra warmth in unheated frames in spring. Use a fine plastic or wire mesh screen to keep birds out of frames when they are open in summer: also to keep birds, cats and other pests away. Also to break the force of strong winds.

If you build your frames according to the diagram, you can back them up against each other, thus providing a mini-greenhouse for yourself.

In larger gardens there are other uses for frames too. The British have lightweight aluminium frames which you can move round the garden, covering a crop to get it started, then moving it on to start another crop—really little more than an overgrown cloche or tent. Or you can make or buy tubular aluminium hoop and plastic tents in all sizes from cloches to greenhouses.

Another practice used by British market gardeners is to put greenhouses on wheels. They're raised six inches off the ground on wheels, and put on railroad track. A semi-rigid skirt is used to seal them at ground level. Once one crop is finished the greenhouses are just wheeled along to cover a new area while a new crop is started.

Combine the two ideas, and you've got a frame on wheels. If you've

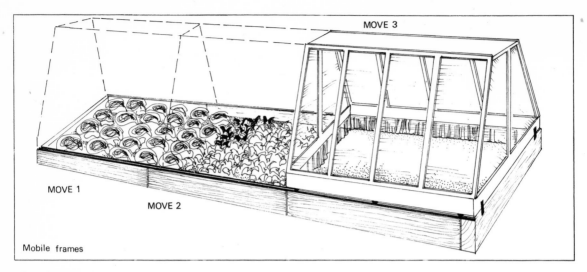

MOVE 3

MOVE 1

MOVE 2

Mobile frames

already got raised beds, and if you used railway ties to raise them, just fix track to the railway ties, and push your frame along whenever you need to. Start a succession of crops keeping the mobile frame over the bed area for two to four weeks per crop before moving it on.

Greenhouses

The same basic principles of east-west orientation and angling of the glass to catch maximum sunlight and heat apply to greenhouses as to frames. So if you skipped the part on frames because you want a greenhouse, go back to the beginning of the chapter.

A greenhouse is really just an overgrown frame, large enough to walk into, and intended to be heated.

There are many ways of heating greenhouses, but probably the simplest is to place the greenhouse close to the home, and hitch it into the domestic heating system. Beyond that you can use electricity, oil, gas, paraffin, coal, coke—even heaters that burn waste automobile engine sump oil as sources of heat. The best way to distribute the heat is by means of small bore pipes, or, if you're using electricity, by means of a fan heater: this has the advantage of blowing the heat into almost every part of the greenhouse, and of keeping the air moving: few plants will tolerate stagnant air.

Just as important as heating the greenhouse in winter is ventilating it in summer. You can kill your crops just as easily by cooking them in summer as you can be freezing them in winter. If you want to optimise your use of greenhouses and frames buy a book on the subject: they're a world of their own. The best coverage is contained in 'The Complete Book of the Greenhouse', Ian G. Walls, Ward Lock Limited, London.

Otherwise stick to using the greenhouse like a frame: to get seeds away to an early start, for late season and winter cropping.

10 Seeding, Thinning and Transplanting

A seed is a complete plant in embryo. It is just like those delicate little Japanese paper flowers you used to be able to get which, when you dropped them into a tumbler of water, would, seemingly miraculously, unfurl themselves.

That may sound like just a pretty-picture representation of how a seed germinates. It's not. It's almost exactly how a seed germinates. Because a seed is a complete plant in miniature, very neatly folded up inside its seedcase. It needs only two things to start unfurling, like the Japanese paper flower. It needs an even and steady supply of moisture —neither too little nor too much—and it needs warmth.

Just how warm depends on the particular seed. And just how fast it germinates again depends on which seed and at what temperature you sow it. Corn, for example, will come up in 4 days from seeding at a temperature of 75°F/24°C. Raise the temperature to 100°F/38°C or more and it won't come up at all. Drop the temperature to 50°F/10°C and it will take 12 days instead of 4 to come up. Drop it to 40°F/4·4°C and it will never come up at all. That's a typical pattern for a warm-season crop. In some areas you may have to wait till midsummer's day for the soil temperature to reach the optimum germination level: if that's the case, start the seed indoors, under frames or in a greenhouse.

Cold season crops are tolerant of cold soils. Lettuce seed, for example, will take 49 days to germinate at 32°F/0°C. It will actually germinate if you embed it in a lump of ice. On the other hand, raise the soil temperature to 70°F/21°C, and it will germinate in a mere 2 days. Raise it to 95°F/36°C and it will never come up at all. Thus, though you can sprout lettuce seed out of doors at relatively low temperatures, you'll get a quicker return by starting the seed at higher temperatures.

But if you just want to get on with the straightforward business of growing good vegetables in your backyard, this is how you do it.

Check on the planning chart, or against the individual vegetable in Part Two, and find out whether it is Hardy, Half-hardy or Tender.

Hardy vegetable seed: germinate at between 50°F–65°F/10°C–18°C.

Half-hardy vegetable seed: germinate at between 50°F–85°F/10°C–29°C.

Tender vegetable seed: germinate at between 65°F–85°F/18°C–29°C.

Which begs the question: how do you know when the soil has reached the required temperature? The simple answer is, you don't. But, broadly, only sow hardy seed out of doors. Soil should have reached 40°F/5°C two weeks after your last official frost, and about 50°F/10°C a month after your last official frost. In unheated frames it will reach these temperatures about two weeks earlier: in raised bed frames, three weeks to a month earlier. Clay soils will be as much as a month later than your area average, sandy soils about a week earlier.

More accurate measurements can be obtained by buying a soil thermometer. Alternatively, consult a good climatological atlas which will show you the soil surface temperature month by month.

Or sow seed indoors, which gives you an earlier start and greater control of temperatures.

Sowing Seeds Out of Doors

First prepare your seedbed. Rough dig the soil in autumn, working in any compost or organic manure you want at that time. Once the ground is frost free in spring, fork the top few inches over lightly. Then level and rake, breaking down any clods. Use the rake too, to remove stones, twigs and other debris. When ready, the soil should have the top two inches loose and crumbly in texture. Don't work it till it's so fine you could pick it up in a vacuum cleaner. It'll turn to mud as soon as it rains if you do that, and when the sun comes out will bake so hard no seed could ever get up through it. Ideally the soil should break down in crumbs, not powder, when you rub it in your hands.

Check depth to plant. Open slit to depth required for seeds: check on planning chart to see how deep seeds should be planted, and plant ac-

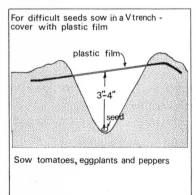
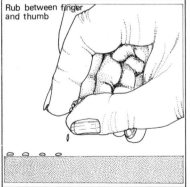
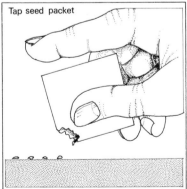

Different methods of sowing seeds

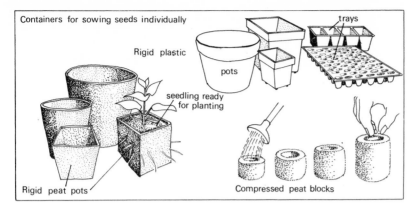

cordingly. Cover lightly, drawing soil back over V–slit with the back of a rake or with a hoe. Firm lightly.

With very shallowly planted seeds, especially those that take a long time to germinate, it is important to keep the sprinkler moving over the rows. If the seeds dry out they may never come up.

Label every row clearly with a tally, telling you what the crop is, and the date on which you planted it.

Sowing Seeds Indoors

Many crops, especially those that need high temperatures for seed germination or which have a long growing season are best started in frames, greenhouses or in the home.

Sow seed indoors (which includes greenhouses and frames) in a soilless growing mix. Use pots or flats if you like, but they do have one disadvantage. You are going to have to disturb the roots when you transplant them: any root disturbance causes a setback to the plant. So better than flats or pots are compressed peat pots, trays or strips. Fill these with soilless growing mix and sow seed to the correct depth. Young seedlings will romp away. Once roots start showing through the sides of the peat blocks, then it is time to plant out. Just open a hole in the bed and put the plant in, peat pot and all. This way you get no root disturbance, no check to growth.

There are many small propagators designed for use by home gardeners in their homes. The simplest of these consists of a plastic tray with a clear plastic dome which you stand on a specially supplied hotplate. Most such designs raise the temperature inside the case 41°F/ 6°C above the ambient temperature of the room in which you stand them. They are perfect for use in the home. Neat, clean, no mess, no bother. You can put a small thermometer inside the case to find out the temperature. With cases like these you have little in the way of problems of seeds drying out.

If you haven't got a propagator like this, but want to germinate seeds indoors, use a grit tray. Plant your seeds in it in peat pots or strips, then

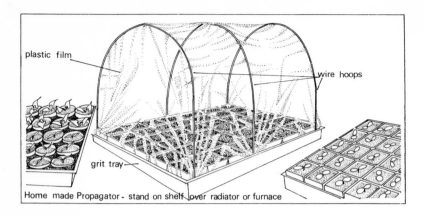

plastic film

wire hoops

grit tray

Home made Propagator - stand on shelf over radiator or furnace

put hoops of wire over the top, and wrap the whole thing in clear plastic film. Stand it on the furnace, or on a shelf over a radiator. If you adopt this procedure it is particularly important to take the temperature of the case inside the plastic: you may find the furnace or radiator is pushing the temperature up too high.

Hardening Off
Seeds raised under glass or in propagators are grown 'soft': that is, they have been raised under very sheltered conditions. Take them straight out into the garden and they will perish. They need to be 'hardened' to withstand outdoor conditions.

Hardening is to plants what weaning is to mammals. You do it by gradually getting them used to colder air than that in the propagator or frame. Propagators usually have vents you can open, increasing the amount of ventilation little by little. With the do-it-yourself models of plastic film over wire hoops, make a few holes in the plastic, then more holes, then more holes again. Then remove the lid of the propagator or the plastic film altogether. Finally move them to a sheltered position outdoors. Still keep the seedlings protected: keep them close to a house wall for extra warmth. Put a pane of glass at a slant over them at night when light radiation frosts may occur. If severe frost threatens, move them into a frame, or even back indoors for the night—but put them in the coldest part of the house.

Transplanting
Seedlings should be hardened for two weeks out of doors before being set in the soil. If you've grown them in a light, sandy growing mix, such as a soilless growing mix, don't put them straight into heavy clay and expect them to keep growing well. Dig plenty of light sandy soil into the planting position. Open a hole with a trowel large enough to put the peat pot or root ball in without having to squeeze or distort it. Return surface soil and make firm. Water lightly.

Protecting Seedlings

Even at this stage of their growth, most seedlings are still vulnerable to extremes of weather. Sudden drops in temperature, even if the air doesn't drop to freezing, can check growth severely: other extremes of weather can check growth and even kill young seedlings: very cold winds—very strong sun. Take protective measures.

The best plan is to cover the young transplants with what the British call cloches and the Americans, tents/hot-caps. These will keep cold winds off the plants, protect them from frost, but accentuate the damage done by suddenly excessively hot sun. Use a shading material, such as lime painted on the sunny side of the cloche to provide protection against sun, but only when the sun is strong. Otherwise don't use it. The seedlings need all the sun they can get.

There are two types of cloche generally available, glass or plastic. The glass ones are probably best for the plants. They're made up in segments, each segment consisting of a wire framework into which you slot the two panes that make the pitched roof, and the two side panes, which also slope, but far more steeply than the roof. One advantage here is that you can remove roof panes to increase ventilation when temperatures rise suddenly. It's also useful if you can remove the roof panes because it means you can harden the plants still further. It gives them less of a shock than if you suddenly whip the whole lot off one sunny afternoon. The main disadvantage of glass tents or cloches is that you have the problem of broken panes, the problem of storing the panes when not in use, and usually the problem of remembering where on earth you stored the wire framework when next you want to use them.

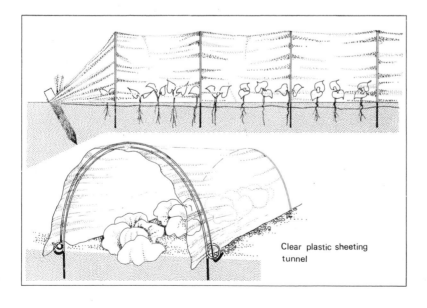

Clear plastic sheeting tunnel

The best alternative is the plastic tunnel: it does the same job as a glass cloche or tent. Just push half-hoops of 11 gauge wire into the soil over the seedlings, and lay plastic sheeting over the hoops, pulling it taut. Cut the sheeting 1 ft/30 cm wider than you need it. Lay one side first. Lay 6 in/15 cm flat on the ground and cover with earth or bricks to weight it down, stretch the plastic sheeting taut over the hoops, then use the other spare 6 in/15 cm the same way on the other side, weighting it down to secure it. If you want to seal the ends of the tunnel, just gather the plastic sheeting together, tie a knot in it, string it to a tent peg and hammer the tent peg into the ground. If you do this both ends it helps to keep the sheeting taut. Alternatively, tidy the ends of the tunnel, looping the sheeting round the end half-hoops and stapling it to itself, and then seal the ends with a sheet of rigid plastic or glass. The advantage of this method is that you can then ventilate when you need to, or keep the tunnel ventilated and merely seal it when severe frosts threaten.

Strong sun and high winds both dry out soil. So keep an eye on soil moisture levels. If soil seems to be drying out, watering is needed. But check first: it may be only the top $\frac{1}{2}$-in/1·3 cm of soil that has dried out. Push a trowel into the soil, and see if it is still moist at the bottom.

Feeding Transplants

It pays to feed transplants 2–3 weeks after planting out. Use a mixture of balanced artificial fertilizer to give instantly available food and organic manure to give a mulch and slower feeding. The mulch effect helps to prevent soil drying out. Apply the mixture either in 6-in/15 cm wide strips down each side of the rows, coming no closer than 3 in/7·5 cm each side of the seedlings or, with big growing plants, put the mixture in a ring round the plant, again coming no nearer to the stem than 3 in/7·5 cm. Make the band of mixture 1 ft/30 cm wide.

Keep transplants protected for their first two to three weeks out of doors. After that keep them growing well.

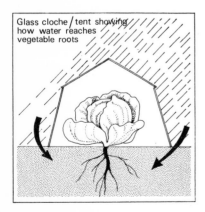

Glass cloche/tent showing how water reaches vegetable roots

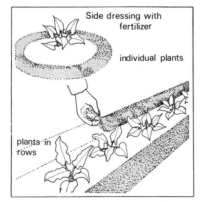

Side dressing with fertilizer

individual plants

plants in rows

11 Cultivating the Crop

While some vegetables have special cultural needs—like tomatoes need tying and some cucumbers need pollinating—all vegetables have certain basic cultural requirements: they all need competition from weeds kept down; they all need an adequate supply of moisture in the soil; they all need measures taken to protect them from pests and diseases.

Keeping Weeds Down

Weeds are always a problem in the vegetable garden. If you're growing vegetables in open ground, every time you turn the soil you bring up more weed seeds. They were buried too deep to germinate: you bring them to the surface and they germinate. They may have lain there since the death of Jefferson or the birth of Victoria, undisturbed: you bring them to life simply by cultivating your plot of land, the main purpose of which is to keep weeds down.

For some reason weeds always manage to germinate faster and grow faster than your vegetables. In doing so they rob your vegetables of valuable water and plant foods. If you let them grow enough they'll smother your seedlings completely.

So how do you keep them down?

There are three ways. The first is chemical. You may use selective pre-emergence weedkillers. They can be very effective, but precisely which chemicals home gardeners can use keep changing: so if you want to use this technique, consult your local county horticultural officer or your state experimental agricultural station.

The traditional way of keeping weeds down is to use a hoe. Use a Dutch hoe with a push-pull action, cutting the weeds off about an inch/ 2·5 centimetres under the surface of the soil. Use a hook hoe with a drawing and pushing motion, again penetrating the soil only about an inch/2·5 cm. Keep the hoe moving between the rows and between the plants throughout the growing season. Use it at least once a week.

A modern approach to weed control is the use of mulches. These suppress weeds. Suitable materials for mulching are peat, well rotted compost, spent hops, basic slag, sawdust, pine needles, ground pine bark or black plastic sheeting. Such mulches not only keep weeds down,

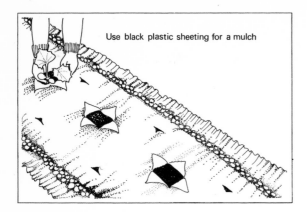

Use black plastic sheeting for a mulch

they also conserve soil moisture by slowing the rate of evaporation.

Watering
All plants need roughly equal parts of water and air in the soil—so make sure the soil is always moist—but never at the extremes of dryness or wetness. Use a moisture meter to check soil moisture levels if in doubt. And read the chapter on 'Water and Watering'.

Pests and Diseases
The longer a plant has been in cultivation, and the more widespread it has become across the globe, the more pests and diseases are likely to attack it. That's life. And since vegetables have probably been cultivated longer than almost any other plants, they have a fair number of enemies. But take heart: the English oak is prey to some 800 diseases, any one of which could cripple or kill it, yet there are thousands upon thousands of fine, sturdy oaks all over the English countryside.

There's a whole chapter devoted to 'Troubleshootin'' which shows you what to do against what. Modern gardeners have found that you can keep the incidence of pests and diseases down by carefully selecting which crops you plant next to which. Such plantings are not completely bug-proof, but they certainly lower the incidence of problems.

For example:
    Chives or garlic near peas or lettuce keep down aphids
    Marigolds near cucumbers and squashes keep down cucumber beetle
    Nasturtiums near broccoli keep down aphids
    Rosemary, sage, thyme, nasturtium, catmint or hyssop near cabbages keep down cabbage-white butterflies
    Tansy near cabbages keep down cabbageworms and cutworms
    Tomatoes near asparagus keep down asparagus beetles.
Keep them down, but do not completely prevent or destroy them.

12 Troubleshootin'

You've heard of the balance of nature. Forget it. It's rubbish. There is no balance in nature. Only a perpetual struggle for dominance between species, animal and vegetable, some of which occasionally enter passing phases of equilibrium. Man, though he'd all too often like to pretend he's above such petty squabbles, is just one of the multitude of animals struggling for dominance. And there are a great many other creatures that enjoy eating the things he enjoys eating. Especially his vegetables.

Some of them are animals. Like rabbits and mice. Many are insects in their various stages of development—eggs, caterpillars, butterflies and moths. Others, curiously enough, are vegetables, like moulds and fungi and bacteria.

But not all animals and insects are threats to your vegetables. Many of them are working on your side. Chalcid wasps, for example, lay their eggs in caterpillars which would otherwise eat your vegetables. This has two advantages. The wasp eggs hatch out inside the caterpillar (whose carcass provides a well-furnished larder for the wasp grubs) thereby killing the caterpillar: at the same time raising another generation of wasps to kill yet more caterpillars. So don't assume too quickly that anything that creeps or crawls over your vegetables is your natural enemy. Get to know your friends and enemies: see below.

Forethought
Before you even plant a vegetable seed, consider what you are going to do on the day when you finally do discover some destructive bug on your beans. Are you going to reach for the nearest pesticide aerosol spray? Are you?

Think before you do.

One of the ironies of our modern society is this: if you want arsenic to kill the worms on your lawn you have to sign the poison register, yet you can walk into any garden centre and buy off the shelf chemicals ten or fifteen times more lethal. There's a whole arsenal of these chemicals waiting for you: pay your money and take your pick. If you dare.

Consider this point: the poisons used by gardeners in the old days were well known. So were the symptoms of poisoning by them. If you sprinkled arsenic on the lawn and licked your fingers, the symptoms showed up pretty soon, and whether you lived or died depended on how many of your fingers you had licked.

The modern gardener's arsenal works far more insidiously, which is not perhaps surprising when it is remembered that many of the modern chemicals were originally developed as nerve gases for use in trench warfare. Make no mistake: the original research work was done to kill people, not garden pests.

There are two main groups of these modern chemicals: the chlorinated hydrocarbons (things like DDT, dieldrin and aldrin) and the organic phosphorus insecticides (such as malathion and parathion). They both have one thing in common: they are based on the carbon atom, and the carbon atom is the basic building block of all life. Start messing around with that, and you do not know where matters will end.

Yet some things have been carefully documented. The modern poisons don't kill you on the spot. They work away at you slowly, insidiously, without you knowing it. The chemicals are stored in the fatty tissues of the body, the kidneys, liver, ovaries, testes, mammary glands and so on. What is frightening is that more is stored than is absorbed. For example, as little as 1/10th of 1 part per million of DDT consumed in the diet, results in the storage in the fatty tissues of 10 to 15 parts per million. That may seem too trivial an amount to worry about, but in experiments with animals it has been established that as little as 3 parts per million will inhibit the production of an enzyme essential to heart action. And none of us knows just how many parts per million of DDT or any other chlorinated hydrocarbon we are walking around with stored away in our fatty tissues. There are young mothers in America, themselves seemingly perfectly healthy, who produce milk from their own mammary glands which contains a higher level of DDT than that considered fit for human consumption in cow's milk.

It's worth bearing in mind, too, that most chlorinated hydrocarbons can remain in the soil for 20 years without measurable degeneration. Plants, you recall, are made up mostly of water, and as they drink up that water they absorb minerals from the soil: some chlorinated hydrocarbons could be among those minerals. You just do not know how much of that deadly spray has got into your vegetables. No one knows.

So ask yourself whenever you reach for an aerosol spray, is it worth the risk? Are you going to reach for one of the cans in this deadly arsenal every time you see a bug in the garden? Are you going to go round letting off these lethal sprays in all directions?

The case against them is not yet proven. But use them with caution. Even at their most harmless, some of them can undoubtedly make you very ill indeed. Yet you are caught in a trap: it is almost impossible to raise worthwhile crops of some vegetables without using chemicals to protect your plants against pests and diseases.

Prophylactic Measures

In gardening, as in medicine, prevention is better than cure. The best way of beating the bugs is not to have any. And the best way of setting about achieving that end is good garden hygiene.

That means keeping the weeds down, not just in the vegetable patch, but all over the garden. Weeds provide a perfect breeding place for most pests and diseases.

Remove rotting vegetation, twigs, yellowing cabbage leaves, things of that sort: they attract pests and diseases.

Grow the right plant in the right place. A healthy plant growing strongly is far less likely to be attacked than a sickly plant. So weed out the sickly specimens, even if it means shortfall on your harvest or making a hole in your tidy rows.

Grow disease-resistant varieties wherever these are available. There are more and more of these for more and more vegetable crops.

Use only disease-treated seed. Again, this is becoming more and more commonly available.

Rotate crops, even those that are not particularly disease-prone.

Know your friends and encourage them.

Grow companion crops: like tomatoes next to asparagus to control asparagus beetle. See the chapter 'Cultivating the Crop'.

Dealing With Bugs

The first thing to do when you come across a bug on your eggplant or tomato is to see whether he's on his own, or whether he's brought his family along too. Watch him for a while: see whether he is chewing or sucking the vegetable leaves, or whether in fact he is eating the aphids you hadn't noticed were there. Take a good look at him (it helps to carry a hand lens to enlarge him), then rush back to the house and try to identify him. Whatever you do, don't kill him till you're sure he's an enemy. What could be more stupid than killing a friend?

Assuming He's an Enemy

If he proves to be an enemy there are several options open to you. Work through them, and only take drastic steps when drastic steps are called for. Start with the mildest measures first.

Harmless Materials The mildest measure you can take against any grub is to squash him between finger and thumb. You can get rid of a relatively large population of bugs by this method. If, however you don't like getting your fingers dirty, try some of these.

Water This well-known, innocuous, colourless, odourless and theoretically tasteless, commonplace liquid can be used with lethal effect against many bugs. Squirt under high pressure—through a hose, syringe or spray gun, at the enemy, and it'll wash them off the leaves onto the soil. They won't climb back up the plant and risk facing the water cannon a second time. They'll probably perish on the soil before they find another host plant. Many clinging bugs will simply be drowned by this treatment. Highly effective against aphids, greenfly, blackfly and many others.

Vegetable Oils These are handy substances: most people have them in the house all the time. Use corn oil, blended cooking oil, castor oil, or one of the proprietary products available from some garden centres. Either spray onto the bugs with a spray gun, or wipe on with a rag. Kills bugs by preventing them from breathing. Deteriorates quickly, leaving no adverse effects on plants or soil.

Milk Another commonplace household commodity, deadly to most bugs. Use as for vegetable oils. Kills by the same means.

Relatively Safe Materials These are relatively safe materials to use, and have the advantage of degenerating very rapidly once used.

Derris Better known in America as Rotenone, it is made from the ground up roots of the derris plant. Use it against sucking and chewing insects. Safe for man and pets, but highly toxic to fish.

Pyrethrum Made from the pyrethrum plant, a relative of the chrysanthemum. Use it against any pests on vegetables. (In general garden use do not use it on any member of the chrysanthemum family.) Like Derris, safe for man and pets, but poisonous to fish.

If you have pest problems, don't use only Derris or only Pyrethrum: use first one, then the other. You get better results that way.

Bordeaux Mixture This old-fashioned concoction, originally developed by the French for use against fungus infections in vineyards, is undergoing a considerable return to popularity. It is a copper-based fungicide. Use it as a safe and effective treatment for fungal infections. Especially useful against mildew. Usually bought as a wettable powder, dissolved in water and then applied through a spray gun.

Ultimate Deterrents These are man-made chemicals, the majority being derived from substances originally developed for use as nerve gases. They can be dangerous to man, beast and fish, as well as the pests against which they are used. Only use them when you really need to. Never use them on vegetables within 2 weeks of anticipated harvest.

Gamma BHC/Sevin/Carbaryl These three are considered the best replacement for the now outlawed DDT. Usually applied as a powder from a puffer-pack or through a spray gun. Being a powder, tends to drift in the wind. Use with caution against pests in general.

Malathion Probably the most deadly of the currently available organo-phosphorus compounds, this is a liquid, usually applied by means of an aerosol. A highly effective wide spectrum pesticide.

> **WARNING Keep all garden chemicals—even ones you consider safe—out of reach of children, preferably in a locked cupboard. Keep them in their original containers. Follow manufacturer's instructions to the letter. Never leave empty containers lying around: get rid of them fast. If you do not have a regular refuse collection, bury them deep. Never burn them.**

America's Top Ten Crop Spoilers

NAME	CROP	CONTROL
Aphid	Eats almost anything	Pyrethrum or malathion
Leafhopper	Eats almost anything	Carbaryl or malathion
White Fly	Most crops: beans and tomatoes usually worst affected	Malathion, once a week for 4 weeks usually cleans crop
Cabbage Looper	Attacks cabbage family	Carbaryl weekly
Colorado potato beetle, Mexican bean beetle, Bean leaf beetle	Beans, eggplants and peppers	Carbaryl, diazinon or methoxychlor dust or spray weekly as needed
Cucumber beetle (striped, spotted and diabrotica)	Cucumbers, marrows, melons, peppers and squashes	Carbaryl, diazinon or methoxychlor dust or spray weekly as needed
Flea beetle, Blister beetle	Peppers, potatoes and tomatoes	Carbaryl, diazinon or methoxychlor dust or spray weekly as needed
Cutworm	Works at night. Cuts young plants at ground level	Carbaryl spray or dust on crops, or diazinon on soil before planting
Squash bug, squash vine borer	Cucumbers, melons, pumpkins and squashes	Carbaryl applied at 10 day intervals
Corn earworm, corn borer	Corn	Carbaryl applied to silks from the time they appear till they brown at 2 – 3 day intervals. For borers, dust foliage

13 Harvesting and Storing

When summer's gone and the dead days of winter are upon you, your vegetable patch looks bleak and blank, wild winds whip with icy fury over them, the earth is like concrete and the water like stone, you can still enjoy garden fresh vegetables. It's easy. All you need to know is how and when to harvest them, and how to store or freeze them.

Harvesting

In Part Two of this book, where you'll find instructions on growing the individual vegetable crops, you'll also find the right time to harvest each crop. In general terms, harvest a crop when it is ripe: in a few cases harvest it just before it is fully ripe: it'll be tastier and more tender then. Once harvested, all vegetables should be washed. One reason is to get rid of any grit that may have got onto or into them as a result of rain or water splash, another is to wash off any chemical sprays or powder residues there may be on them. Do this for all vegetables, whether you are going to eat them straight away, store them, freeze them.

Storing Vegetables

Most of the vegetables the home gardener grows can be stored successfully given the right conditions. These are—darkness, coolness (temperatures around 32°F/o°C), high humidity (about 85 to 90%), and good ventilation.

The likeliest places to find such conditions are a cellar or crawlspace: failing that a well-insulated attic or unheated garage or garden shed may do.

Construct yourself a chest-of-drawers structure using 2 by 1 in/5 by 2·5 cm slats. Cover the outside with hardboard. Nail fine-gauge chicken wire over the outside as protection against birds, mice and so on. Then make the drawers. These should be quite deep, anything from 6 in/15 cm to 1 ft/30 cm. Make the bottom of the drawers of fine-gauge chicken wire or extruded plastic netting to allow for good air circulation through the vegetables.

Store your vegetables when and as they become ready. Buy yourself a combined hygrometer (which will tell you the relative humidity in the room) and thermometer, so you can check temperatures. Keep humidity between 85–90%. If it drops, sprinkle the floor with water, or keep a wide-topped bowl filled with water in the room all the time. Place the storage stand near a window, and keep this open as much of the time as possible to provide ventilation. Alternatively, keep a fan blowing air round and round the room. Just a fan: no heater.

Most of the vegetables mentioned in this book will store well under these conditions. Exceptions are ripe tomatoes and greens—which will not store long unless frozen—pumpkins, squashes, marrows, onions, peas and beans which store better under cool, dry conditions. If in doubt as to whether a vegetable will store successfully: don't.

Freezing

This is rapidly replacing the cool storage of vegetables for winter use, and rightly so, since vegetables properly prepared and frozen are a joy to eat, months after they were harvested.

Freeze the vegetables in season when and as they are harvested. Procedure is simple.

Sort the vegetables according to size, unless they are to be sliced or cut into chunks later. Wash thoroughly in cool water to rinse out any soil or sand particles or bugs. Cut large vegetables like turnips or swedes into square chunks, long vegetables like beans into slices. Then blanch them. This is the most important operation in freezing vegetables. It arrests enzyme action in the vegetables which were the blanching not done would continue, destroying the taste and texture of the vegetables. It consists of boiling the vegetable in question for a very specific length of time. Use a blanching pan if you have one: otherwise use a deep fry pan and basket. Use one pint/half a litre of water for each pound/half a kilogram of vegetables to be blanched. Blanch small quantities rather than large quantities at each blanching. Bring the water to the boil, and keep it boiling over a hot flame: place the prepared vegetables in a basket. Plunge them into the boiling water and put the lid on the pan. Start timing. Different vegetables need to be blanched for different lengths of time. Any good book on freezer cookery will tell you. If you live over 5,000 ft/1,660 m above sea level, add 1 minute blanching time to the recommended time. As soon as the blanching time is up, lift the basket and vegetables out of the boiling water and plunge straight into very cold water, preferably cold running water. Leave them there for the same number of minutes as you blanched them. Once cooled, allow them to drain.

Once they're drained, put them into their freezer containers. Plastic bags are the usual containers. Once in their bags, it is important to get rid of as much air as you can from the bag. The more air left in the bag the more quickly the frozen food will deteriorate. Ideally frozen foods should be stored under vacuum conditions. There are three ways you can get rid of most of the air in the bags. The first is to close the neck of the bag as you would if you were going to blow it up, only instead you slip a straw inside and suck the air out. The second is to do this with a small vacuum pump specially designed for this purpose: this is both more efficient and more hygienic. The third method is to lower the filled bag slowly into cold water: the weight of the water pressing against the side of the bag will push most of the air out. Once you've created your vacuum, seal the neck of the bag, label it, and place it in the freezer.

The label should state the name of the vegetable and the date on which it was placed in the freezer. It helps if you keep a chart on the side of the freezer telling you what vegetables you froze on what dates, and when you removed them. That way you can see at a glance what you have in the freezer at any moment in time. The records also help you to know whether you could have done with more of this or less of that, and then to grow more or less accordingly.

Frozen properly, most vegetables will be a joy to eat as much as 8 or 12 months later. After that, taste and texture may begin to deteriorate. Ideally, try to maintain a complete turnover of vegetables in your freezer every year.

Part Two
14 How to Use Part Two

Now you know the basics of home vegetable growing, the time has come to meet the crops. A pretty formidable lot they can seem. Look at any well-managed vegetable plot and you could start quaking in your shoes, wondering how on earth anyone could know enough to grow so many different plants with so many different needs so successfully.

Since all you need to succeed with vegetables are facts, these are summarised in data-sheet form at the top of each individual vegetable entry. Here's what the data sheet parts will tell you.

The Name of the Vegetable Both the English and the American common names are given.

Latin name This is given because often there are confusions between American and English common names. Besides, if you keep seeing the same generic name popping up, you'll know that some of that vegetable's needs are the same as for others with the same generic name.

Hardiness The vegetables in this book are all rated as Hardy, Half-hardy or Tender. The ratings correspond with the zone maps in this book. A Hardy vegetable is Hardy in the Hardy zone. A Half-hardy vegetable can be grown out of doors in the Half-hardy zones but needs to be started indoors in the Hardy zone, and so on. It's all explained on the zone maps.

pH ideal This is the figure at which the vegetable can be expected to give of its very best. Don't worry if you're a point or two the wrong side. Most vegetables are very tolerant of soil pH variations. The ones that aren't are noted. On the other hand don't expect a first rate crop from a vegetable with a pH ideal of 7·5 if your soil is way off the mark—like pH 5.

Depth to sow Crucial information. There are probably more disappointments among vegetable gardeners because they planted seed the wrong depth than for any other reason. Too deep and seed will never have the energy to reach the surface: too shallow and they'll dry out before they've had time to germinate. It's important to sow seed the right depth.

When to sow Just as important as how deep to sow. Seeding times are usually given in relation to your first or last frost date. If the instruction is 'sow seed 2 weeks after your last frost', check your last frost date with the maps and take it from there. Your last frost date is the date on which officially your last frost should occur. Only it would become so boring repeating the 'official' all the way through. It doesn't mean you have to stand out there in your shirtsleeves in the cold taking the temperature of the night air.

Seeds per foot This is related to the percentage of seed you can expect to germinate and the number of plants you would normally want per ft/30 cm. Sowing more seeds than you need is wasteful: it wastes your time because you've got to thin them out later: it wastes your money because, with few exceptions, seed you don't sow this year is seed you can sow next year. Wasteful too, because we're rapidly heading for a world seed shortage.

Days to germination An important figure for two reasons. The first is that you need to know how long it should take seed to come up when it hasn't come up. There's no point in re-seeding a crop after a week if it normally takes that crop 3 weeks to show through the ground. The second reason is that if you want to use a pre-emergence weedkiller, you can only do it on crops that take over a week to come up.

% germination This tells you what percentage of the seed you sow should come up. The figures are official. They are the minimum percentage germination required by law. In most cases you'll get a higher germination rate. Where the germination rate is considerably higher a + sign has been added.

When to plant outdoors This tells you when to plant out seedlings, regardless of whether the seedlings are home grown or garden centre transplants.

Space between plants This tells you how much space to leave between each plant. You'll find the distances given slightly smaller than in most other books. There are two reasons for this. The first is that, as gardens get smaller and the need to grow vegetables gets greater, you've just got to pack the plants in more closely. The second is quite simply that in most cases you'll get a better crop by growing the plants closer than normally recommended.

Space between rows This tells you how far apart to space the rows. You must have a space between the rows so you can move up and down them when you're weeding, feeding and harvesting them.

Yield per plant The figures given are averages. Try to do better.

Plants per person Most people plant far too many of most vegetables. On average, one third of the plants in the vegetable patch get wasted. Try to plant only what you need. The figures given here are based on average shopping habits. They also only expect you to eat the vegetables fresh. If you're going to freeze them, double the figure. Multiply up for the size of your family. If you've got a family of 4 multiply the given figure by 4. Individual tastes vary: you'll find from experience that you'll want more of some vegetables and less of others. Keep records, and correct the figures over 2 to 3 years.

Days to harvest Very important. It's hopeless trying to grow a crop that takes 170 days to mature if your growing season is only 120 days. Check on the zone map to make sure you have a long enough growing season for the vegetable you want to grow. Less important in the UK, where you can't tell summer from winter and most crops labelled Hardy will stand through winter, than in the USA where summer is summer and winter is winter.

Life of seed Most people buy seeds afresh each year, and just throw away what they don't use. In fact the seeds of most vegetables are viable for several years. Just how long you can keep the seed of any particular vegetable is a closely guarded trade secret: after all, the seed-merchants want you to keep buying new seed each year. Reduce the germination rate by 10% for each year you store the seed: 10% for 1 year: 20% for 2 years, and so on.

Varieties Both British and American varieties have been included. Your best guide as to which varieties will do well in your zone will be found in seedsmen's catalogues. Keep an eye on current catalogues, and keep abreast of the gardening press. That way you'll always be ahead of everyone else with new varieties and varieties better suited to your season length.

15 The Vegetables

Beans

Beans, English Broad or Fava	Varieties
LATIN NAME *Vicia faba*	**BUSH**
HARDINESS Hardy	'The Midget'
pH IDEAL 6·2	**POLE**
DEPTH TO SOW 2½ in/6·3 cm	Early: 'Aquadulce'
WHEN TO SOW November for spring crop in Half-hardy areas and/or 4 weeks before last frost for early summer crop	Late: 'Imperial White Longpod' 'Imperial Green Longpod'
SEEDS PER FOOT 5–8	
DAYS TO GERMINATION 7–14	
% GERMINATION 75	
WHEN TO PLANT OUTDOORS —	
SPACE BETWEEN PLANTS 3–4 in/7·5–10 cm	
SPACE BETWEEN ROWS 18–24 in/46–60 cm	
YIELD PER PLANT 2 oz/58 gms	
PLANTS PER PERSON 48	
DAYS TO HARVEST 80–90	
LIFE OF SEED 3 years	

These are not a bean at all. Come to that they're not quite a pea either. They belong to the vetch family which should suggest to you, if you were brought up on a farm, that they might make excellent cattle fodder. They are usually grown as a substitute for Lima or butter beans, so it's the seeds you eat, but if picked young enough the whole shell can be steamed till tender and eaten that way. Easy to grow, very hardy and very rich in protein and vitamins.

Soil English broad or Fava beans like a deep, rich, well worked soil. Use a soil that has been manured for a previous crop, not a newly manured soil. Apply no manure or fertilizers before planting. They like the soil rather more alkaline than most plants, so when working the soil dig in hydrated lime at the rate of 4 oz/112 gms per sq yd/m².

Seeding In Half-hardy areas sow seeds in the ground around your first frost date. Choose a sunny, sheltered situation. A sowing in November will produce a crop around your last frost date: useful since few other vegetables will be in season. In Hardy zones sow seed 4 weeks before your last frost for an early summer crop. The Longpod varieties are best for overwintering: the Windsor varieties for spring sowing. Seeds are large so take care how you sow them: if you just drop them into a dibble hole they'll stick halfway down with an air hole underneath them. Nothing grows that way. Take out a hole with a trowel and seat the bean seed securely at the bottom of it. Plant seeds 3–4 in/7.5–10 cm apart in rows as little as 9 in/23 cm apart for spring sowing, then cover 2 rows at a time with barn cloches or plastic tunnels to get the seeds away to a good start.

Transplanting Unnecessary.

Cultivation Use a hoe to keep weeds down between the plants. Keep a moderate level of moisture in the soil. Once plants are well into growth, stick twigs into the ground for the beans to clamber up. They're not true climbers but you'll get a better crop if the beans can lift themselves off the ground. Since the plants have a poorly developed root system, earth up round the bases of the stems, hilling only 2–3 in/5–7.5 cm high to keep the plants more securely in the ground. At the same time work in a 6–9–18 (low nitrogen) fertilizer at the rate of 3–4 oz/sq yd: 87–112 gms/m².

Harvesting Pick the pods when they are about 6 in/15 cm long if you want to use them as a substitute for snap beans. Let them grow on to their full size and ripen before picking if it's the seeds you want to use. After harvesting cut the plants off at ground level: put the tops on the compost heap. They're chock-a-block with nitrogen: just what compost bins need. So are the roots, but unless you need to use the land immediately (in which case they can follow the topgrowth into the compost bin), dig these into the soil and let them rot.

Mistakes to avoid English broad or Fava beans are a cool season crop.

They'll produce nothing if you try to grow them through the heat of summer, so always sow early or late. The Windsor varieties have the best flavour but don't crop well if grown through the short winter days.

Beans, Snap, French, Kidney or String	*Varieties*
LATIN NAME *Phaseolus vulgaris*	BUSH
	'Royalty'
HARDINESS Tender	'Romano 14'
pH IDEAL 6·8	'Devil Fin Precoce'
	'Canadian Wonder'
DEPTH TO SOW 1½ in/3·8 cm	'Bush Blue Lake'
WHEN TO SOW After danger of frost/6 weeks earlier under glass	'Golden Waxpod'
	'Tendercrop'
SEEDS PER FOOT 6–8	
DAYS TO GERMINATION 6–14	POLE
	'Kentucky Wonder'
% GERMINATION 80+	'Romano'
WHEN TO PLANT OUTDOORS 8 weeks after last frost	'Blue Lake'
	'Stringless'
SPACE BETWEEN PLANTS Bush 2–3 in/5–7·5 cm	
Pole 4–6 in/10–15 cm	
SPACE BETWEEN ROWS Bush 18–30 in/46–75 cm	
Pole 36–48 in/1–1·2 m	
YIELD PER PLANT 1 oz/29 gms	
PLANTS PER PERSON 56	
DAYS TO HARVEST 60–80	
LIFE OF SEED 3 years	

When Americans talk about bush beans, these are the ones they mean, though there are pole varieties too. They're the perfect small garden crop, giving more edible produce per unit area used than any other vegetable. They're easy to grow provided you get the soil right: the bush varieties need no staking, the pole varieties will grow happily up 4 ft/1·2 m twigs placed along the rows when plants are about 3 in/7·5 cm high. Natives of North America, they like sun, sun and more sun. They've never heard of frost—so don't try introducing them to the idea.

Soil Choose a sunny situation in the vegetable garden and unless your soil is already light and sandy work in plenty of coarse sand and clinkers and some peat or compost to lighten the soil. At the same time work in a 6–9–18 or 10–8–10 artificial fertilizer at the rate of 3–4 oz/sq yd: 87–112 gms/m². Organic fertilizers such as farmyard manure, cottonseed waste or dry blood will help heavy cropping.

Seeding 3 ways you can do this. Either start seed indoors up to 6 weeks before your last frost date: or sow out of doors where plants are to grow after all danger of frost. Or sow at your last frost date under cloches or plastic tunnels. If starting indoors, place the seeds at the sunniest window in the house or use artificial light with a time clock set to give a 16 hour daylength. Keep seeds and seedlings moist but never wet.

Transplanting Plant out seedlings 3–4 weeks after the last frost in Half-hardy areas, up to 8 weeks after last frost in Hardy zones. Water seedlings well in, then keep an eye on them to make sure a crust does not form on the soil surface round them.

Cultivation Keep the hoe moving between the rows all through the growing season. Nothing cuts the crop down so much as a compacted soil over the roots. Don't think that watering will solve compacted soil problems: it will merely rot the roots. After harvesting the first crop, apply 10–7–10 fertilizer at the rate of 2–3 oz/sq yd: 58–87 gms/m² in 3 in/7·5 cm bands each side of the crop. Don't let the fertilizer touch the crop itself or it will burn it. Hoe the bands into the soil then water well in. This way you'll get a second crop—not so heavy as the first crop, but still worth having, especially in small space gardens.

Harvesting Harvest the beans while they are still young and succulent. A bean in perfect picking condition should snap when you break it. If it doesn't, it's too old to bother with. Harvest carefully, cutting the beans from the plant. Don't try to pull them off the plant: chances are you'll pull the whole plant out of the ground. The beans mature at high speed: one day there's hardly a sign of a bean on the bush: a week later the crop is overripe. So watch the plants daily from flowering time on, otherwise you won't catch the beans at their best.

Mistakes to avoid Planting too early outdoors: seeds will not germinate in cold soils, and transplants set out in soil that is too cold will suffer a severe setback and could perish. Planting too deep: indoors, under cloches or outdoors in early spring plant only 1 in/2·5 cm deep. Later in the season plant 2 in/5 cm deep. Crusting over of soil: beans just never push their way up through a crusted soil. Mulch with peat or compost to make life easy for the beans. Failure to feed the crop: don't forget to work fertilizer into the soil before planting. Beans make rapid growth and need plenty of readily available nutrients if they are to grow away well and crop well. Failure to water: beans that are allowed to dry out abort. The first few beans will ripen but the rest will shrivel.

Beans, Butter, Lima or Madagascar	Varieties

LATIN NAME *Phaseolus lunatus (= limensis)*

HARDINESS Tender

pH IDEAL 6·0

DEPTH TO SOW $1\frac{1}{2}$ in/3·8 cm

WHEN TO SOW 4 weeks after last frost

SEEDS PER FOOT Bush 5–8

Pole 4–5

DAYS TO GERMINATION 7–12

% GERMINATION 70

WHEN TO PLANT OUTDOORS 6 weeks after last frost

SPACE BETWEEN PLANTS Bush 3–6 in/7·5–15 cm

Pole 6–10 in/15–25 cm

SPACE BETWEEN ROWS Bush 24–30 in/60–75 cm
Pole 30–36 in/75–90 cm

YIELD PER PLANT 2 oz/58 gms

PLANTS PER PERSON 48

DAYS TO HARVEST 90–100

LIFE OF SEED 3 years

Varieties

BUSH
'Fordhook 242'
'Comtesse de Chambord'
'Henderson Bush'
'Thaxter'

POLE
'Goliath' (= 'Prizetaker')
'King of the Garden'
'Challenger'

Lima or butter beans are grown for their edible seeds, not for their pods. They are even more tender than snap beans, need a warmer soil for the seed to germinate and a longer growing season for the pods to ripen fully and for the beans to achieve their full size. In spite of which they are not a hot weather vegetable and in extremely hot summers fail to set pods. There are both bush and pole varieties.

Soil Choose a sunny situation in the garden and, unless your soil is already a light one, dig in plenty of sand or cinders, together with a little peat or compost. At the same time work in a 10–7–10 fertilizer at the rate of 3–4 oz/sq yd: 87–112 gms/m². Organic manures also help heavy cropping, but avoid manures with a high nitrogen content. It's the P and K these beans put to best use.

Seeding Sow seed indoors as for snap beans or in frames, preferably heated, around your last frost date. If direct sowing outdoors, sow 4 weeks after your last frost. Cover with barn cloches/plastic tents to get

Young Brussels sprouts developing

A well-grown head cabbage ready for harvesting

Red cabbages like these are often known as pickling cabbages

Dwarf curly kale—a reliable winter vegetable for colder districts

the seedlings off to a good start. Keep seedlings moist but never wet, and never let the soil crust over. A 1 in/2·5 cm layer of moss peat will usually be sufficient to prevent crusting.

Transplanting Plant out seedlings 3–4 weeks after the last frost. Keep them under cloches/plastic tents for a further couple of weeks to keep them growing well. Any sudden frost or a wind with a high chill factor could kill the lot even at this stage. Open the cloches or the ends of the plastic tents every day for about a week before removing them. If sudden late frosts or high chill-factor winds threaten don't hesitate: put those cloches or plastic tents back at once.

Cultivation Keep the hoe moving between the plants. The one thing Lima beans can't stand is a crusted soil. So keep it open (but take care not to slice the roots off the plants in your eagerness. It's all too easily done.) 4 weeks after planting out, apply a 10–7–10 fertilizer at the rate of 2–3 oz/sq yd: 58–87 gms/m² in 3 in/3·8 cm strips 6 in/15 cm either side of the rows, hoe in then water in. Keep the crop moist but never wet. Most bush varieties can be grown on pea sticks put into the ground as soon as the cloches/tents have been removed. Pole varieties should be planted round poles already set in the ground. Do this when preparing the soil. There's a right and a wrong way to string the poles. The British, being of a conservative character, do it the wrong way: just part of a longstanding tradition handed down through generations. The Americans do it the right way: not hampered by unchangeable tradition, they had to think it out, so they thought it out right. Make a double-T pole 9 ft/3 m tall. Put 3 ft/1 m in the ground leaving 6 ft/2 m above ground. Take strings or wires from the outsides of the Ts to the base of the pole. Plant the beans close to the strings at the base of the pole. As they grow up the pole the beans will hang downwards and outwards. This helps them grow long, straight: it also helps them ripen and makes them easier to harvest.

Harvesting These are a long-season crop so leave the beans on the plant as long as you possibly can. Harvest about 1 week before your first frost. Beans picked earlier will be smaller and more tender. Some people prefer them that way. Tender young beans can be used like snap beans: mature beans should be shelled, then dried or frozen.

Mistakes to avoid Planting too early: these beans are even more sensitive to cold soils and cold weather than snap beans. Letting the soil crust: stops seedlings getting through, impedes growth of the plant. Failure to supply sufficient nutrients before planting: means the beans grow slowly in the early stages. Too much nitrogen: means the beans make all leaf growth and don't set their beans soon enough before the frosts set in.

Beans, Runner	Varieties
LATIN NAME *Phaseolus coccineus*	BUSH
HARDINESS Half-hardy	'Brezo'
	'Hammonds' Dwarf
pH IDEAL 6·2	Scarlet'
DEPTH TO SOW 2–3 in/2·5–3·8 cm	
WHEN TO SOW 3 weeks after last frost	POLE
SEEDS PER FOOT 4–6	'Streamline'
	'Enorma'
DAYS TO GERMINATION 6–14	'Achievement'
% GERMINATION 75	'Prizewinner'
WHEN TO PLANT OUTDOORS 2 weeks after last frost	
SPACE BETWEEN PLANTS 4–6 in/10–15 cm	
SPACE BETWEEN ROWS 36–48 in/1–1·2 m	
YIELD PER PLANT 2 lbs/1 kg	
PLANTS PER PERSON 10	
DAYS TO HARVEST 60–70	
LIFE OF SEED 3 years	

Grown in America almost exclusively as an ornamental vine, this bean is one of the staple crops of the British home garden. Popularly known as the scarlet runner bean, there are several varieties with white flowers: both planted together are more decorative than simply one or other. There are both bush and pole varieties. The bush varieties are excellent for small space gardens, but the yield and quality of the beans are often disappointing. The pole varieties are the tallest-growing of all beans, ramping up to 12–15 ft/4–5 m with good cultivation. In full leaf and full pod the vines are very heavy, so make sure the supports you put in are stout, strong and secure in the ground.

Soil Unlike other beans, runner beans do best in a freshly manured soil. Prepare the soil by taking out a trench for each planting row 10 in/ 25 cm deep and a spade's width across. Break up the soil at the bottom of the trench and add in 2–3 in/5–7·5 cm of compost or well-rotted manure plus hydrated lime at the rate of 2–3 oz/sq yd: 58–87 gms/m². Dig this into the bottom of the trench, then return the soil to the trench, trampling down till firm. Then add a 10–7–10 artificial fertilizer at the rate of 2–3 oz/sq yd: 58–87 gms/m² and dig this into the soil you just returned to the trench. Leave for 2 weeks then insert the poles. A series

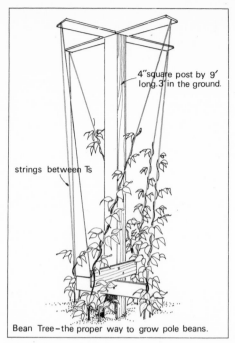

4"square post by 9' long. 3' in the ground.

strings between Ts

Bean Tree – the proper way to grow pole beans.

of single T-poles set straight down the centre of the row, tied across the top by a single 2×3 in/5×7.5 cm piece of hardwood and supported by angle bars at each end will usually hold the crop securely. Poles should be 16 ft/5 m tall, with 4 ft/1.2 m buried in the ground. Strings or wires should run from the outer edge of the Ts to the base of the poles.

Seeding Sow seed in open ground, one at the foot of each string. Plant 2–3 in/5–7.5 cm deep. Plant 6 or 8 spare seeds at the end of the row to transplant later should any fail to germinate where you want them. If all seeds germinate along the poles, put the spares in the compost bin.

Transplanting Not necessary except when seeds fail to germinate at the foot of the strings. Then transplant with a trowel disturbing the roots as little as possible. Time to transplant is about 3 weeks after sowing. By then you should know whether all or none of your main sowing has germinated.

Cultivating Give the plants a 1–2 in/2.5–5 cm mulch of compost or peat as soon as the plants are 3–4 in/7.5–10 cm tall. Keep well watered but never wet. The beans climb by twining: tie any dangling shoots back onto the strings with raffia. As soon as the first beans start to form, give a 4–5 in/10–12.5 cm mulch with strawy manure or use a 6–10–18 artificial fertilizer at the rate of 2–3 oz/sq yd: 58–87 gms/m² applied in 3 in/7.5 cm bands 3–4 in/7.5–10 cm away from the plants on the side away from the poles. Fork lightly in, then water well. From then on ensure that the soil has a high moisture content, otherwise the beans will become stringy. Spray the beans overhead at dusk or dawn: this not only helps the flowers to set and so form beans, it also helps keep the beans tender.

Harvesting Harvest the beans when they are three-quarters of the length the catalogues claim they will grow to. If you let them grow full length expect stringy beans. You'll get less beans per plant by harvesting them earlier, but you'll be able to eat all of every bean you pluck.

Mistakes to avoid Allowing the soil to dry out: leads to stringy beans. Also causes flowers to fall, in which case you get no beans at all. Overplanting: most people overplant. Runner beans are heavy bearers. 10 plants per person is fine if you're going to freeze half the crop: otherwise stick to 5 plants per person.

Cabbages

Cabbage	*Varieties*
LATIN NAME *Brassica oleracea* var *capitata*	SUMMER HARVEST
HARDINESS Hardy	'Golden Acre'
pH IDEAL 6·5	'Avoncrest'
DEPTH TO SOW ½ in/1·3 cm	'Resistant Red Acre'
WHEN TO SOW For summer harvest: 6 weeks before transplant date. For fall and winter harvest: 4, 8 and 12 weeks after last frost	'Green Express' 'Greyhound' 'Primo' 'Red Acre'
SEEDS PER FOOT 8–10	FALL AND WINTER HARVEST
DAYS TO GERMINATION 7–12	'January King'
% GERMINATION 75+	'Early Head'
WHEN TO PLANT OUTDOORS 2–8 weeks after last frost	'Winter Monarch' 'Celtic'
SPACE BETWEEN PLANTS 12–20 in/30–50 cm	'Cheiftan Savoy'
SPACE BETWEEN ROWS 24–30 in/60–75 cm	'Savoy King'
YIELD PER PLANT 1 lb 6 oz/665 gms	
PLANTS PER PERSON 5	
DAYS TO HARVEST 60–150	
LIFE OF SEED 4 years	

Cabbages are one of the easiest and hardiest of vegetables you can grow. By nature they are biennials, forming their good, firm round heads the first year, then shooting up into flower the second year. It's the round head produced the first season that you eat: just for curiosity, leave one plant in the ground to see what a cabbage looks like in flower.

Soil Cabbages are greedy feeders, particularly demanding on nitrogen, so prepare the soil well to a depth of about 1 ft/30 cm digging in plenty of manure or compost together with 3–4 oz/sq yd:87–112 gms/m² of 12–6–6 artificial fertilizer. Work the fertilizer well into the soil, otherwise it could burn the roots of seedlings and transplants.

Seeding Cabbage seed can be sown at almost any time of year to produce a harvest at almost any time of the year. For best results sow seed in several batches. Make the first sowing 6–8 weeks before your last frost, planting seed only $\frac{1}{2}$ in/1·3 cm deep. That will give you a good crop in early summer. For fall and winter crops make sowings 4, 8 and 12 weeks after your last frost. Alternatively, sow a small number of seeds at fortnightly intervals from your last frost date on, using transplants for your early crop.

Transplanting Seeds are normally sown where the plants are to grow. Transplants, however, are by far the best way of getting a good early crop. Buy transplants with stems no more than the thickness of a pencil and set them in the ground 20 in/50 cm apart in rows 36 in/1 m apart. Beware of buying transplants with thicker stems. You might expect them to mature more quickly—but you could be in for a surprise. Large transplants, with the head already well-formed are liable to bolt if temperatures drop to below 50°F/10°C for more than a couple of weeks. So stick to small transplants. They're best value in the long run.

Cultivation Keep the plants weed-free by hoeing or using a mulch. Keep an eye on soil moisture content: it does not need to be high but cabbages grown under drought conditions are not a good cook's favourite. Feed the plants about 4 weeks after planting out or thinning out (use the thinnings as greens) by applying ammonium nitrate/nitrochalk at the rate of 1 oz/sq yd:29 gms/m². Throughout much of the UK it has now become virtually impossible to grow cabbages unless you take stringent precautions against cabbage root flies. Routine control is with calomel paste. The problem here is that the cabbage root flies are laughing at most modern chemicals. Solution: be old-fashioned. Put a plastic collar round the cabbage stem. You'll get a 95–100% success rate—which is far higher than any chemical will give you.

Harvesting Simply pluck the plants from the ground. Cut the roots off and use them in the compost bin.

Mistakes to avoid The commonest mistake with cabbages is planting too many: usually far too many. Plant only what you know you can use in a 2–3 week period in any one seeding.

Broccoli	*Varieties*
LATIN NAME *Brassica oleracea* cvs.	'Green Sprouting'
HARDINESS Half-hardy	'Waltham 29'
pH IDEAL 6·5	'Green Comet'
DEPTH TO SOW $\frac{1}{2}$ in/1·3 cm	'Calabrese'
WHEN TO SOW 3 weeks after last frost	
SEEDS PER FOOT 10–15	
DAYS TO GERMINATION 7–12	
% GERMINATION 75+	
WHEN TO PLANT OUTDOORS 4 weeks after last frost	
SPACE BETWEEN PLANTS 14–18 in/35–46 cm	
SPACE BETWEEN ROWS 24–30 in/60–75 cm	
YIELD PER PLANT 12–16 oz/340–435 gms	
PLANTS PER PERSON 5	
DAYS TO HARVEST 60–100	
LIFE OF SEED 3 years	

Broccoli is one of the members of the cabbage family grown for its edible flowers rather than for its leaves, though it still comes under the rather vague term 'greens'. It's more closely related to the cauliflower than the cabbage, the main difference being that in the cauliflower the flower is produced in a compact head, whereas in broccoli it is produced in a series of loosely formed side-shoots. It is a perennial plant, though usually grown as a biennial. If left in the ground it can be harvested over several seasons. The problem is that it will grow taller with the passing years, and become increasingly hideous as it rises above the surrounding vegetables. At best it is tall growing and so needs a position sheltered from strong winds which can easily rock it out of the ground. For best results start the crop afresh each year, discarding old plants which can make a more valuable contribution to the compost bin than they can to the table. Broccoli is even hardier than cabbage and can be left standing through the winter. Surprisingly, it is also more heat tolerant than cabbage.

Soil Soil needs are the same as for cabbage: a well-worked soil with plenty of manure or compost dug in and a 6–9–18 fertilizer worked thoroughly into the soil at the rate of 4 oz/sq yd : 112 gms/m².

Seeding Sow seed around the time of your last frost, using a seedbed or sowing where the plants are to grow. Don't waste valuable frame, greenhouse or windowsill space on broccoli seed. It is perfectly hardy. Save frames, greenhouses and windowsills for plants that really need an early start. Seed should be sown $\frac{1}{2}$ in/1·3 cm deep.

Transplanting Even if you sow seed in the soil where the plants are to grow, it'll pay you to lift them and replant them. The reason is this: the plants are tall growing so they need to be set firmly in the soil. This is done by putting them about 1 in/2·5 cm deeper in the soil than they were growing in the flats or seedbed, and then making the soil round them really firm. The best time to set out transplants is 4 weeks after your last frost.

Cultivation Keep weeds down with a 1–2 in/3–5 cm mulch of peat or compost in a ring round the plants or in lines beside the rows. Feed with roughly 1 oz/sq yd : 29 gms/m² ammonium nitrate/nitro-chalk in rings or beside the rows worked well into the mulch about 4 weeks after planting out. For a really good crop side dress with a 12–6–6 fertilizer at the rate of 4 oz/sq yd : 112 gms/m². No special care is needed in cultivating broccoli, except to make sure the soil never dries out.

Harvesting The flower heads are best removed when they are small and not too far developed. They are far more tender when picked young like this. Remove the head at the top first, then pick the side-heads as and when you need them. As you pick them, other side-heads will follow on to replace them. You should be able to keep harvesting from midsummer right through until hard frosts set in. Light frosts improve the taste.

Mistakes to avoid Planting too shallowly is the commonest mistake. Plants then fall over in the lightest breeze. If your soil is very friable (highly desirable) don't be ashamed to stake your broccolis. It may be unconventional—but it works.

Brussels Sprouts	*Varieties*
LATIN NAME *Brassica oleracea* cus.	'Jade Cross'
HARDINESS Hardy	'Peer Gynt'
	'Long Island Improved'
pH IDEAL 6·2	'Topscore'

DEPTH TO SOW $\frac{1}{2}$ in/1·3 cm

WHEN TO SOW 2 weeks after last frost and/or June/July

SEEDS PER FOOT 10–15

DAYS TO GERMINATION 7–12

% GERMINATION 75+

WHEN TO PLANT OUTDOORS 4 weeks after last frost and/or July/
August

SPACE BETWEEN PLANTS 12–18 in/30–46 cm

SPACE BETWEEN ROWS 24–30 in/60–75 cm

YIELD PER PLANT 1 lb 4 oz/547 gms

PLANTS PER PERSON 5

DAYS TO HARVEST 100/110

LIFE OF SEED 5 years

'Achilles'
'King Arthur'

Sprouts are probably best described as an aberrant type of cabbage which, instead of producing a large single head of leaves, produces dozens of tiny, tight little heads in the leaf axils all the way up the stem. An extraordinary arrangement, but very useful because the yield is so high. Useful too, because in Half-hardy zones they will bear right through the winter.

Soil You can grow sprouts in literally any fertile soil. You can grow it in almost pure sand, almost pure gravel and in heavy clay. Problem is, in poor soils you'll get a poor crop. The plants will grow long and leggy, and produce loose-leaved sprouts. If you're going to grow sprouts at all take the trouble to grow them well. Prepare the soil exactly as for cabbages, trenching 10 in/25 cm deep and working in plenty of compost or manure as well as 4 oz/sq yd : 112 gms/m² of 12–6–6 fertilizer. If your soil is on the acid side of neutral, apply hydrated lime at the rate of 3 oz/sq yd : 87 gms/m², per planting.

Seeding In cool summer areas such as the UK and the maritime regions of the Hardy zone in the USA make 2 sowings, one about first frost date to mature 12 months later, the other about last frost date to crop in late winter/early spring the following year. In Hardy and Half-hardy zones, make only 1 sowing, about April/May to harvest the same year.

Transplanting Plants should be set out in their rows when they are about 4–6/10–15 cm high. Plant firmly. The topgrowth becomes very heavy once the sprouts start to develop, and the top-heavy plants fall over easily in high winds or heavy rains. If you've made 2 sowings, don't transplant, merely thin: use the thinnings as greens. If you're only aiming at 1 harvest you'd do better to buy in young transplants than grow them yourself. The slight setback they suffer in transplanting helps to make them sturdier and bear sooner.

Cultivation Sprouts will grow perfectly well left to themselves from there on, provided you keep them adequately watered and take control measures against cabbage root fly (see Cabbage). For best results apply a heavy mulch (3–4 in/7·5–10 cm) farmyard manure or compost plus 4 oz/112 gms of 6–10–18 artificial fertilizer per sq yd/m² dug well into the mulch.

Harvesting Sprouts mature from the bottom of the stem up. The way to harvest them is to remove the lowest leaves with a sharp downward tug, then gather the sprouts growing at the leaft joints with a gentle twisting action. As the lower leaves and sprouts are removed, so those higher up the stem will mature in sequence. In cold winter areas the sprouts will be ruined if they are left on the plant once the freeze starts, so make sure you harvest them all before this happens. The way to be sure you can do this is to pinch the growing tip out of the plant in early fall. All the sprouts will then mature at the same time. This probably means that you will have to grow less sprouts than you would in milder winter areas, so don't overplant.

Mistakes to avoid Planting too early or too late. Too early and the crop will wither in summer: it won't stand summer heat. Planting too late in cold winter areas simply means the crop won't be ready to harvest before the freeze sets in.

Cauliflower	*Varieties*
LATIN NAME *Brassica oleracea*	'Snowball'
HARDINESS Half-hardy	'Snow King'
pH IDEAL 6·5	'Polar Bear'
DEPTH TO SOW $\frac{1}{2}$ in/1·3 cm	'All The Year Round'
WHEN TO SOW Indoors: 6 weeks before transplant date	'Asmer Snocap'
Outdoors: 2 weeks after last frost	
SEEDS PER FOOT 8–10	
DAYS TO GERMINATION 7–12	
% GERMINATION 75+	

WHEN TO PLANT OUTDOORS Last frost date

SPACE BETWEEN PLANTS 18 in/46 cm

SPACE BETWEEN ROWS 30–36 in/75–90 cm

YIELD PER PLANT 10 lbs/283 gms

PLANTS PER PERSON 5 plants

DAYS TO HARVEST 60–100

LIFE OF SEED 4 years

Cauliflower is probably the finest of the cabbages grown for the flower rather than for the leaves. Indeed, when well grown it is one of the finest of vegetables. The general cultivation of the cauliflower is the same as for the cabbage, but it is altogether a rather more difficult plant to grow well. It won't stand as much cold as cabbage, and it won't head up properly in hot summer regions. It has, incidentally, been developed more highly than most vegetables over the past centuries. An illustration in a seventeenth-century English book shows it with a flower no bigger than a golf ball: an English golf ball at that.

Soil Prepare the soil by taking out a trench 10 in/25 cm deep and a spade's width across. Work in plenty of manure or compost plus 4–5 oz/sq yd: 112–145 gms/m² of any commercial 10–7–10 fertilizer. Lime at the rate of 4 oz/112 gms per sq yd/m².

Seeding Sow seed in position 2 weeks after your last frost or up to 6 weeks earlier indoors, under frames or in the greenhouse. Sow small quantities at 2 week intervals, otherwise you'll have the whole crop maturing at the same time.

Transplanting Only sow indoors if you want an early crop. Transplants should be set in the ground at or just after your last frost date. Set them 18 in/46 cm apart in the rows, with rows 30–36 in/75–90 cm apart.

Cultivation Take standard cabbage root fly precautions (see Cabbages) or you could loose 90% of your crop. Keep the weeds down with a good mulch of compost. 6 weeks after planting out apply a follow-up feed of 1 lb/435 gms ammonium nitrate/nitro-chalk per 100 ft/33 m of row. Work this follow up feed well into the mulch, then water heavily. As soon as the curds (heads) start to show, start blanching. This is far easier than with most vegetables that need blanching. All you do is gather the leaves together over the curd and tie them in position with a tough rubber band or a piece of raffia. Leave for 7–10 days, then harvest; if left the heads are inclined to run to seed rather quickly.

Harvesting Pluck the plant from the soil, slice off the root, untie the leaves gathered over the curd, cut them back to half their length. Root and leaf trimmings are excellent for the compost bin.

Mistakes to avoid Overplanting and planting too close together in the rows.

Kale	Varieties
LATIN NAME *Brassica oleracea*	'Blue Curled Scotch'
HARDINESS Hardy	'Dwarf Green Curled'
pH IDEAL 6·5	'Dwarf Siberian Curled'
DEPTH TO SOW $\frac{1}{2}$ in/1·3 cm	
WHEN TO SOW 3–4 months before first frost	
SEEDS PER FOOT 8–10	
DAYS TO GERMINATION 7–12	
% GERMINATION 75+	
WHEN TO PLANT OUTDOORS 4 weeks before last frost	
SPACE BETWEEN PLANTS 8–12 in/20–30 cm	
SPACE BETWEEN ROWS 18–24 in/46–60 cm	
YIELD PER PLANT 1 lb/435 gms	
PLANTS PER PERSON 6	
DAYS TO HARVEST 55–65	
LIFE OF SEED 5 years	

Kale is yet another derivative of the ubiquitous common European cabbage. Its chief merit is that it is extremely hardy, and it is often grown as 'winter greens', since it will survive frost drop levels that turn most other cabbage-type crops to slush. It has never been the most popular of vegetables since, certainly compared with other cabbage-type plants, it's rather strong-tasting. Extremely frost-hardy, the one thing it can't stand is summer heat. So grow it as a spring or fall crop. The fall crops are usually the best.

Soil Plant in well-dug soil that has been manured for a previous crop, never in freshly manured ground. Not too fussy as to soil pH or texture, probably does best where nutrient levels are high but balanced: use a 10–7–10 fertilizer at the rate of 2 oz/sq yd : 58 gms/m².

Seeding Sow seed for fall crops 3–4 months before your first frost date. Sow the seed at the rate of 8–10 per ft/30 cm, then thin to 8–12 in/20–30 cm between the plants. Use the thinnings in salads. Spring crops can be sown around first frost date in the UK and in seaboard areas of the Half-hardy zone in the USA.

Transplanting Not necessary except for spring crops. The best spring crops are those grown from transplants. Set them in the ground 8–12 in/20–30 cm apart 4 weeks before your last frost.

Cultivation Simply ensure that the soil never dries out. Keep weeds down with a mulch of compost or any other low-nutrient content organic substance.

Harvesting Pluck the leaves from the plants with a sharp downward pull. Gather leaves as needed. After harvesting put the haulms and roots in the compost bin.

Mistakes to avoid Trying to grow a good crop in summer heat.

Corn

Corn	*Varieties*
LATIN NAME *Zea mays*	'Golden Bantam'
HARDINESS Tender	'Snow Cross'
pH IDEAL 6·5	'Polar Vee'
DEPTH TO SOW 2 in/5 cm	'Northern Belle'
WHEN TO SOW Indoors 10–12 weeks before transplant date	'Sprite'
SEEDS PER FOOT 4–6	'Silver Queen'
DAYS TO GERMINATION 6–12	
% GERMINATION 75+	
WHEN TO PLANT OUTDOORS 4–6 weeks after last frost	
SPACE BETWEEN PLANTS 10–14 in/25–35 cm	
SPACE BETWEEN ROWS 30–36 in/75–90 cm	
YIELD PER PLANT 2–6 ears	
PLANTS PER PERSON 15	
DAYS TO HARVEST 60–100	
LIFE OF SEED 3 years	

The art of growing corn to its sweet, plump perfection seems, like happiness, to be an inalienable American birthright. If you're British and the only corn you've ever tasted came from a supermarket or out of a packet from the supermarket deepfreeze, shatter your taste-buds by growing corn the way the Americans do. The only real problem you'll run into is that corn is a hot summer, long-season crop and it doesn't take kindly to those dull grey muggy British summers that you can only distinguish from British winters by checking the calendar. You'll only ripen the ears in the UK if you grow short-stature fast-maturing variet-ies. New ones are being developed all the time, so keep a keen eye on catalogues and latest developments in the gardening press.

Soil Corn likes a light sandy soil. If you haven't got a light sandy soil set about improving it the fall before you want to plant. Trench the ground 12–18 in/30–46 cm deep and dig in plenty of coarse sand, clinkers and peat: alternatively use an inert substance like perlite or vermiculite to lighten the soil. At the same time, dig in barrowloads of compost or manure. Leave overwinter. In spring add 3–4 oz/sq yd: 87–112 gms/m² of 10–7–10 fertilizer, digging this well into the top 10 in/25 cm of the plot. When preparing the soil, remember that corn grows best in blocks, not rows. It's a grain crop. It's wind pollinated. If you plant in rows and the wind decides to blow straight across the rows instead of straight along them, you could finish up with none of the ears getting pollinated. Incidentally, if you're unfamiliar with corn, a few tips on terminology could come in handy. The male flower is called the tassel. It occurs right at the top of the plant. The female flowers occur on the same plant but lower down the stem: they are called ears. The ear is covered by modified leaves which are called the husk. Between the husk and the tip of the ear there are some long threads called the silk. In fact they are the styles of the female flowers and it is they that must receive the pollen from the tassel if edible ears are to be produced.

Seeding In the USA sow seed 2 in/5 cm deep out of doors where the plants are to grow. Rate of seeding should produce seedlings 3–4 in/ 7·5–10 cm apart. Make successive sowings in different blocks every 2–3 weeks for a continuous harvest from summer through fall. Or plant early, mid and late varieties all at the same time. In the UK, sow seed indoors in a heated greenhouse, frame or on the windowsill of a warm room in full sun in early March. Sow seeds in peat pots in soilless growing mix, 2 seeds per pot. Once they've germinated pluck out the weaker of the two seedlings.

Transplanting Not applicable in the USA. In the UK keep the plants growing well but gradually harden them. It is important that they never suffer any check to growth. Plant out late May or early June and keep covered with cloches for 4 weeks, gradually admitting more and more air to the cloches. Finally remove the cloches.

Cultivation Two problems here. First, feeding. Then thinning. Corn is a fast grower and a greedy feeder, so make sure at all times that there is plenty of fertilizer available for it to make growth. At seeding time apply 4 oz/sq yd: 112 gms/m² of 10–7–10 fertilizer, preferably in 3 in/ 7·5 cm bands each side of the plants. When the corn is 8–10 in/20–25 cm high, (straight after transplanting in the UK) apply 1 oz/sq yd: 29 gms/m² of any 12–6–6 fertilizer in rings or bands. Repeat the dose again when the corn is 18 in/46 cm high. If you spot nitrogen deficiency (you can see it at a glance: the leaves go yellow) rush to your nearest garden centre for a nitrogen-only fertilizer and apply in bands at the rate of 3 oz/sq yd: 87 gms/m². Thinning is the other problem. You raise all those corn seedlings, then discard three-quarters of them. It goes against the grain. Harden your heart. It's necessary. More home grown corn crops are ruined by overcrowding of plants in the plots than any other single factor. Surplus seedlings have the same food robbing properties as weeds—so get rid of them. Be ruthless. You'll get more good ears if you are. Ideally plants should be 10–14 in/25–35 cm apart. If in doubt, err on the side of overspacing rather than over-crowding. Keep weeds down with a good mulch of strawy manure or compost. Never hoe the soil round the corn. You'll kill it. Apart from that, you must keep the corn growing right through the season. That means water, water, water all season. Then double the water supply from tasselling time to harvesting: that's when corn most needs its water. Forget the water and you might as well forget the corn: it'll be hard and tasteless.

Harvesting This is the moment that matters. The acid test, when you know whether you're a good corn grower or just a ham. Problem is usually to know just when to pick the ears. First, watch the silks. They start life a light whitish-green. As the ears ripen the silks darken. In some varieties they go dark brown, in others, black. But silk texture is an important as colour. Dark brown moist silks show ears that are ready for plucking. Dry, matted silks show you missed the moment for picking. Watch the husks too: they should be dark green at harvest time. The perfect moment to pluck corn is when the kernels have filled and spurt 'milk' if you puncture them with your thumbnail. But don't try that right across the crop: you won't have a kernel left fit to eat if you go on that way. Try it on one or two ears: match the moment to the silk colour and harvest the rest by silk colour. Now comes the crunch: corn is at its sweetest the moment you cut it from the plant. Within 10 seconds the sugars have started to turn to starches. Moral: have the water boiling in the pot before you cut the ear. Don't boil corn for more than 5–6 minutes otherwise you boil the flavour away. Alternatively keep the corn cool and moist till you're ready to cook it—up to 48 hours later. Don't remove the husk till you're right ready to cook. If you remove the husk when you pick the corn the kernels will taste like sawdust.

Mistakes to avoid In the UK the commonest mistake is planting out the corn too early in the hope of giving it a long growing season. If you get it off to a good start under glass you've already beaten the season length problem. In the USA the main mistakes are removing suckers (seldom seen in the UK) in the belief that they are taking goodness from the parent plant. Not true. Controlled experiments prove that in fact you get a better yield if you leave the suckers on the plants. De-tasselling: this is done in the belief that you get a better yield if you remove the tassels once the ears start to swell. Again, controlled experiments show it doesn't make the slightest difference to yield. So save your time and keep watering the corn. Failure to take prophylactic action against corn earworm: varieties with tight husks suffer less damage from corn earworms than other varieties.

Cucumbers, Squashes, Melons and that Lot

Cucumber	*Varieties*
LATIN NAME *Cucumis sativus*	SLICING
HARDINESS Tender	'Ashley'
pH IDEAL 7	'Marketmore'
	'Burpee Hybrid'
DEPTH TO SOW 1 in/2·5 cm	'Triumph Hybrid'
WHEN TO SOW 4–6 weeks before transplant date	'Burpless Green King'
SEEDS PER FOOT 3–5	PICKLING
DAYS TO GERMINATION 6–14	'SMR 48'
% GERMINATION 80+	'Pioneer'
WHEN TO PLANT OUTDOORS 4 weeks after last frost	
SPACE BETWEEN PLANTS 12 in/30 cm or 3 plants per hill	
SPACE BETWEEN ROWS 48–72 in/1·2–2 m or 5 ft between hills	
YIELD PER PLANT 4 lbs/2 kgs	
PLANTS PER PERSON 1	
DAYS TO HARVEST 55–75	
LIFE OF SEED 5 years	

Cucumbers have been cultivated for so long no one's quite sure any more where they came from originally. Most people think India. That's likely, especially as they are recorded as having been cultivated in China (which got many of its food plants from India) as much as two and a half thousand years ago. On the other hand, the French found them being cultivated in what is now Montreal, and De Soto found them being cultivated in Florida. It's one thing to cross the Himalayas, but how did cucumbers get from the Old World to the New World so long before Europeans got there? Perhaps by some long-ago forgotten migratory or trade route via the Aleutians. Who knows. Who cares. Here's how you grow them.

Soil Cucumbers aren't fussy about soil so long as it's 90% humus. No joking. Some of the best cucumbers ever grown were simply planted straight on top of an old compost bin. You can do that provided the compost bin is in full sun. Most people grow them in hills. Start preparing the hills in the fall. Dig a hole 3 ft/1 m deep, 3 ft/1 m across and dunk 1 ft/30 cm well rotted farmyard manure or compost in the bottom. As you fill back the soil, mix in more manure or compost so that what goes back to make the hill is 50/50 original soil and compost or manure. Don't worry if the hill looks like a mountain when you've finished. By the end of the winter it will have settled down to looking like a hill. Space the hills 24–36 in/60–92 cm apart and leave up to 5 ft/1·5 m between the rows of hills. If you haven't got room for hills that doesn't mean you have to abandon cucumbers. Train the vine up a fence or pole or even the house wall. Or grow mini varieties like 'Pink Patio' or 'Tiny Dill Cuke' in tubs, pots, boxes or even hanging baskets.

Seeding Cucumbers are fast-growing short-season crops but they need plenty of heat. Wherever you live in the States summer comes some time, and when it comes it's hot. That's the moment to grow your cucumbers. In Britain meteorological matters are managed less efficiently: last summer came about 20 years ago. Which means that the cucumbers described here need to be grown in a heated greenhouse in the UK. For pseudo-hardy frame and ridge cucumbers suitable for Britain, simply follow catalogue instructions. Sow seed of USA or greenhouse varieties 1 in/2·5 cm deep, 9–12 seeds per hill, sowing 4–6 weeks after the last frost. Where the growing season is short, sow seed indoors or under glass 4–8 weeks earlier. Once seedlings are up thin to 4–6 per hill: 2 weeks later thin again, leaving only the 2–3 most vigorous on each hill.

Transplanting Transplants should be set out 2–4 weeks after the last frost. They'll still be tender at that stage so cover them with cloches, plastic tents or hot caps. Frame cucumbers can be grown this way in the UK, provided the cloches are kept over the plants through the

A well-managed vegetable garden in late summer

Summer squash or custard marrow

Use small-space plants like parsley or chives for edging borders

whole growing season. Gradually harden off plants and remove cloches/ tents/hot caps.

Cultivation The first thing you need to know when growing cucumbers is that they are 96% water. That should tell you that they need water, water and still more water every day of their growing lives. The second thing you need to know is that they are acutely allergic to artificial fertilizers. So just don't apply any. That's why it is so important to get plenty of good plant foods into the soil before planting. Cucumbers send their roots down deep—as much as 3 ft/1 m. That in turn dictates the way you water. Give the plants a lot of water slowly. A little and often sprinkled over the surface will encourage plants to curl their roots up and then scorch them in the sun. Lots of water delivered slowly soaks deep into the soil where the active feeding roots can use it. The rest is wasted. If the plant is not getting enough water it'll tell you. It'll simply stop growing. If it does that, water it heavily and it will just start growing again from where it left off. Keep hills weedfree with a mulch of compost, shredded pine-bark, coconut fibre or any other high-humus/low-nutrient mulch. Skip all that nonsense about pollinating cucumbers: the ones you have to pollinate taste bitter. Grow only the modern gynoecius (all female) types.

Harvesting The secret of harvesting cucumbers that are fit to eat is to read up how long they ought to grow according to the catalogue, then harvest them when they are half that length. By the time they've reached full length they've lost all their flavour. Besides, the more you harvest the more your plants will produce.

Mistakes to avoid Planting too early; letting the cucumbers grow to full length; insufficient watering.

Marrows and Squashes	*Varieties*
LATIN NAME *Cucurbita* spp.	SUMMER
HARDINESS Half-hardy	'Sweet Dumpling'
pH IDEAL 6·5	'Early Prolific Straight-neck'
DEPTH TO SOW 1 in/2·5 cm	'Zucchini'
WHEN TO SOW Outdoors: 4–6 weeks after last frost	'Vegetable Spaghetti'
Indoors: 3–4 weeks earlier	'Hubbard Golden'
SEEDS PER FOOT Summer: 4–6	WINTER
	'Butternut'
Winter: 1–2	'Gold Nugget'
	'Hundredweight'

DAYS TO GERMINATION	Summer: 5–14
	Winter: 6–12
% GERMINATION	75+
WHEN TO PLANT OUTDOORS	4–6 weeks after last frost
SPACE BETWEEN PLANTS	Summer: 6–24 in/15–60 cm
	Winter: 24–48 in/60–120 cm
SPACE BETWEEN ROWS	Summer: 36–60 in/1–1·5 m
	Winter: 72–120 in/2–3·8 m
YIELD PER PLANT	Summer: 4 lbs/2 kg
	Winter: 3 lbs/1·5 kg
PLANTS PER PERSON	Summer: 2
	Winter: 3
DAYS TO HARVEST	Summer: 50–60
	Winter: 80–120
LIFE OF SEED	4 years

The British call them marrows. The Americans call them summer squashes. Botanically, they're all varieties of the same plant, *Cucurbita pepo*, a native of Mexico and Central America. Winter squashes are slightly different. They're all varieties of *Cucurbita maxima*, natives of the lower Andes, and considerably more tender than the vegetable marrows or summer squashes. Both can be grown out of doors in the UK, but the winter squashes need to be started under glass before planting out, whereas the summer squashes can be sown direct where they are to grow, though they'll do better too if started under glass.

Soil Squashes, or marrows, need much the same general soil preparation as cucumbers. They'll grow to perfection planted straight into a compost bin, provided it's in full sun. Failing that, plant them in hills prepared in the autumn made up almost entirely of compost with a low nitrogen (6–10–18) fertilizer mixed well into the hills at a rate of 4–5 oz/sq yd: 112–145 gms/m².

Seeding Sow seed 1 in/2·5 cm deep where it is to grow in Half-hardy zones 4–6 weeks after your last frost. In Hardy zones sow seed indoors or under glass 3–4 weeks earlier. When sowing indoors press the seeds into the growing mix with the pointed end upwards. Only just cover the seed indoors. Use peat pots so that the plants can later be put out without disturbing the roots. Winter squashes should be sown indoors in the UK, though they'll do fine in the USA where summers warm up much faster.

Transplanting Plant out into hills 4–6 weeks after your last frost. In the UK pot-on winter squashes into 12 in/30 cm pots, tubs or barrels and keep them in the greenhouse or under heated frames through the whole growing season. Seedlings put out of doors must be hardened carefully. Use plastic tents or cloches: even a dunce's cap made of cardboard will serve to keep the chill of the nights off the young plants.

Cultivation Like cucumbers, marrows and squashes are about 95% water, so their prime cultural requirement is plenty of water all through the growing season. They're deep rooting plants, so none of this little-and-often treatment for them. Give them a really good soaking, plenty of water applied slowly so that it can soak right down to where the active feeding roots are growing is what is wanted. Keep weeds down with a good thick mulch of compost, peat, pine needles, pine-bark or any similar material. Plants soon grow too dense to make any further cultivations possible: the large leaves can then take over, making a good ground cover in their own right. Female flowers must be pollinated to produce fruits. The way you do this is to pick a male flower and simply push the centre of the male flower into the centre of the female flower. Female flowers are easily recognisable because they have incipient marrows or squashes behind them. The other flowers are male.

Harvesting This is where the crunch comes and sorts out the summer squashes from the winter squashes. Pick summer squashes and marrows when they're still quite small, about half to three-quarters the length the catalogues say they'll grow to. Keep the plants harvested: the more you pick, the more young fruits will appear. Winter squashes are harvested when they are fully grown—and this—as much as their tenderness—is what makes them so difficult to grow to maturity in the UK. The growing season isn't long enough or hot enough for them. And it's no good picking winter squashes until they are fully mature: picked early they are watery and have hardly any flavour. They need a touch of cold weather, but not direct frost, to bring out the flavour.

Mistakes to avoid Failure to pollinate. Planting too close. All marrows and squashes are big-growers—great sprawly things. In small gardens, train the vines up a fence or pole. Another mistake is to assume you've done something wrong if the first fruits abort. Don't worry. It's just the same as with cucumbers. The male flowers usually open about a week before the female flowers, so there's nothing to pollinate them. Some late season fruits may abort too. This is quite natural. The plant will very sensibly set only as many fruits as it can mature. Aborting is just nature's way of pruning the harvest so it won't overtax the strength of the plant.

Pumpkins	*Varieties*
LATIN NAME *Cucurbita mixta*	'Big Tom' ('Connecticut Field')
HARDINESS Tender	'Cinderella'
pH IDEAL 7	'Small Sugar' (New England Pie)
DEPTH TO SOW 1½ in/3·8 cm	'Bix Max' (the 100 lb pumpkin)
WHEN TO SOW Outdoors: 4–6 weeks after last frost	'Cheyenne Bush'
Indoors: 3–4 weeks after last frost	
SEEDS PER FOOT 2	
DAYS TO GERMINATION 6–14	
% GERMINATION 70	
WHEN TO PLANT OUTDOORS 4–6 weeks after last frost	
SPACE BETWEEN PLANTS 30–36 in/76–91 cm	
SPACE BETWEEN ROWS 72–120 in/2–3·8 m	
YIELD PER PLANT 3–5 pumpkins (20–30 lbs/10–15 kg each)	
PLANTS PER PERSON 1	
DAYS TO HARVEST 75–150	
LIFE OF SEED 4 years	

Pumpkin pie is the American national dish. Which is an excellent enough reason for separating the pumpkin from its allies, the squashes and marrows. But there's another reason too. It's a different species yet again. *Cucurbita mixta,* a native of Mexico and Central America. It is a far more sensitive plant than the squashes, being intolerant of the heat of the southern states and intolerant of the damp chilliness of spring in the northern states. As for the British climate, it's really too cool and chilly to plant out even in the rare years when summers do come, so is best grown in a large frame. National dish though it may be, many American home gardeners find the pumpkin far too large a plant for their gardens. If you find yourself thinking 'that's me', try growing your pumpkins up a trellis, fence or pole. You can grow it in a very small space that way.

Soil As for marrows, squashes and cucumbers, pumpkins need a well-drained soil that's chock-a-block with humus. Make hills about 3 ft/

1 m across from rich compost or well-rotted manure. If the soil is heavy, add in coarse sand, cinders, vermiculite or perlite.

Seeding Sow seed as for squashes. In Tender zones sow direct, putting the seed 1 in/2·5 cm deep and making the sowing as soon after your last frost as the soil reaches 65°F/18°C. In Half-hardy zones sow seeds in peat pots 3–4 weeks before your last frost date. Push the seeds blunt end down into the growing mix—preferably one of the soilless types—and only just cover the pointed tip.

Transplanting Plant out seedlings in their peat pots without disturbing the roots 4–6 weeks after your last frost in Half-hardy zones. In Hardy zones pot them on into 12 in/30 cm pots or, for heavy crops, into tubs or half-barrels to be grown on in frames or the greenhouse.

Cultivation Avoid disturbing the roots by keeping weeds down with a thick mulch of compost, peat, pine needles, shredded bark or sawdust. Then water and water and water. Apply a lot of water to each plant, and apply it slowly so that it can soak right down to the feeding roots 2–3 ft/ 60–90 cm down below. Pollinate as for squashes and marrows.

Harvesting The critical thing here is that you must let the pumpkins ripen on the plants, but you must also get the harvest in before the frosts get to them. Some years it can be a touch-go fingernail-biting business, while you wonder whether your pumpkins or the frost is going to make it first. If frosts threaten before you have harvested the pumpkins, protect them with a layer of sacking overnight when necessary. One of the tricks of harvesting is to cut the pumpkins from the vines, then leave them lying around on the ground for a few days before storing them. This helps to toughen the skins. Don't leave them out for more than a week or you will toughen the skin so much it will feel like rhinohide. On the other hand, if you are only growing the pumpkins for fun at Hallowe'en, really tough skins will do no harm. Overripe pumpkins and pumpkins that have been cut and left out can make you ill: so eat them all at once or deep freeze. Never re-heat pumpkin pie.

Mistakes to avoid Failure to pollinate. Planting out too early in an attempt to give the pumpkins as long a growing season as possible. Some years you'll get away with it, but mostly you'll find there's a late frost, just waiting to catch you beat-the season people out. Overplanting: this may be sheer patriotism in America but is inexcusable in the UK. You don't need more than 1 or 2 plants per person, and you shouldn't try to cram the plants closer together than 12 in/30 cm apart. Most families would probably find that one vine would be quite enough for them.

Melons (Cantaloupes)	Varieties
LATIN NAME *Curcumis melo*	'Gold Star'
HARDINESS Half-hardy	'Early Crenshaw'
pH IDEAL 6·0	'Burpee Hybrid'
	'Iroquois'

Melons (Cantaloupes)   *Varieties*

LATIN NAME *Curcumis melo*

HARDINESS Half-hardy

pH IDEAL 6·0

DEPTH TO SOW 1 in/2·5 cm

WHEN TO SOW Outdoors: 4–6 weeks after last frost (USA only)

Indoors: 3–4 weeks earlier

SEEDS PER FOOT 3–6

DAYS TO GERMINATION 4–12

% GERMINATION 70+

WHEN TO PLANT OUTDOORS 4–6 weeks after last frost

SPACE BETWEEN PLANTS 12–16 in/30–40 cm

SPACE BETWEEN ROWS 60–72 in/1·8–2 m

YIELD PER PLANT 25–30 lbs/12–15 kg

PLANTS PER PERSON 5–15

DAYS TO HARVEST 75–100

LIFE OF SEED 2 years

Melons belong to the same family as cucumbers and gherkins. The main difference when you come to grow them is that melons are basically a tropical plant, while cucumbers are almost hardy. To succeed with them you need hot summers and you need to start them early. Though quite fast-maturing, they must be in full growth by midsummer: the melons just won't ripen in the shorter fall days.

Soil Like marrows, squashes and cucumbers, melons need a soil best described as a hump of humus. Grow them literally on the compost heap or on hills into which all the compost and well-rotted manure you can find has been dug in. Prepare the hills the fall before you want to plant out. Two weeks before planting out turn the hills over, thoroughly mixing in a high nitrogen (12–6–6) fertilizer at the rate of 3–4 oz/ sq yd: 87–112 gms/m². If you live on heavy soil, add plenty of sand, vermiculite, peat or perlite to ensure that the hills will be well drained.

Seeding Seeds should be sown as for squashes and pumpkins, by being pushed blunt end down into the seeding mix and the pointed tips just covered. In Half-hardy zones (except UK) sow seed out of doors 4–6 weeks after your last frost. In Hardy areas and anywhere in the UK sow seed in peat pots indoors 3–4 weeks earlier. Seeds need a temperature of 65°F/18°C plus to germinate.

Transplanting Set transplants out in their hills 4–6 weeks after your last frost. In the UK, try melons out of doors in Gulf Stream coastal areas only. Elsewhere keep them throughout growing season in an unheated frame or greenhouse, or plant against a sheltered south wall in full sun. Leave at least 12 in/30 cm between plants.

Cultivation The rule with melons is a daily dose of water. Water, water, water, from the day you sow the seed through till the last melon has been harvested. Melons are deep-rooting plants, so apply a lot of water slowly to let it soak right down to where the active feeding tips of the roots are: they could be 3 ft/1 m down in the soil. None of this little-and-often watering. That does melons more harm than good. If you plant the hills leaving a hollow in the middle, the simplest way to water is just to leave the hose trickling into a flowerpot placed in the middle of the hollow for 2–3 hours every evening. Mulch the plants to keep weeds down and also to conserve moisture. Use compost, pine needles, peat or black plastic sheeting. 4 weeks after planting out feed the plants again, using a 6–10–18 fertilizer at the rate of 3 oz/sq yd : 87 gms/m². Fork this lightly into the mulch or, if you're using plastic sheeting, into the top 2–3 in/5–7.5 cm of soil under the sheeting. Feed again with the same fertilizer applied in the same way at the same rate as soon as first fruits start to set. You must pollinate the flowers to obtain fruit. Transfer the pollen from the male to the female flowers with a camel hair paintbrush. Female flowers are easy to recognise: there is a slight swelling behind them—the incipient melon. Reduce rate of watering by half as soon as the melons start to ripen.

Harvesting Commercial growers harvest their melons when they are 'full slip', which means that the stem breaks cleanly away from the plant under slight pressure. That's too early to harvest them from your own garden. 'Full slip' harvesting takes into account the time it will take the melons to get to market, and assumes that they'll go on ripening all the way to the supermarket. In fact they merely deteriorate. Harvest your own garden-grown melons when they are vine ripe: that is, when the melon comes away in your hand if you just lift it slightly.

Mistakes to avoid Never overplant. Crowded plants produce fewer and smaller melons. In cool summer regions the few melons they produce will be less likely to ripen. Rushing into planting too early to try to get mature plants by high summer only to have them cut back by late frosts. Planting too late: plants will never mature in time. Day length matters as well as heat.

Onions

More onions, in one or other of their many forms, are grown by home gardeners across the world than any other vegetable. No one knows for sure where onions came from originally, but they've been in cultivation for so long that it's a pretty fair bet that they are natives of the countries of the eastern Mediterranean. That's where food crops were first cultivated in the Old World, and it is from that centre that most of these ancient food plants have spread across the world as man migrated, taking most of his food plants with him. The onion and its forms are bulbs, placed by botanists in a family somewhere between the lilies and the amaryllis. The bulb, often known as a globe, is the part eaten in most forms of onion, but in some it is the leaves. These are peculiar among plants in that, like the flower stem, they are hollow. In some forms the flowers are quite ornamental.

Onion	*Varieties*
LATIN NAME *Allium cepa*	LONG DAY (14–16 HOURS) (UK and Northern USA)
HARDINESS Hardy	
pH IDEAL 6·0	'Bunching Onions'
DEPTH TO SOW ½ in/1·3 cm	'Scallions'
	'Early Yellow'
WHEN TO SOW Indoors: 8 weeks earlier than outdoors	'Sweet Spanish'
	'Ailsa Craig'
Outdoors: Last frost date and/or August for fall crop	'White Lisbon'
SEEDS PER FOOT 10–15	
DAYS TO GERMINATION 7–14	SHORT DAY (12 HOURS) (Southern USA)
% GERMINATION 70+	'Excel'
	'Texas Grano'
WHEN TO PLANT OUTDOORS 1 week after last frost date	'Crystal White Wax'
	'Yellow Bermuda'
SPACE BETWEEN PLANTS 2–3 in/5–7·5 cm	
SPACE BETWEEN ROWS 12–24 in/30–60 cm	
YIELD PER PLANT 4 oz/112 gms	
PLANTS PER PERSON 15	
DAYS TO HARVEST 100–165	
LIFE OF SEED 1 year	

Onions have more culinary uses than any other vegetable. You can eat them raw or cooked; in salads, stews, soups, sauces, pickles, you can fry them, stew them, boil them, even roast them.

Soil Onions need a deep, friable, well-worked soil, yet they are one of those crops that you can grow in the same spot year after year, so once you've done the initial hard work you can go on reaping the reward for years to come. Dig a trench 10 in/25 cm deep and add in all the compost and well-rotted manure you can, as well as 3–4 oz/sq yd:87–112 gms/m² of 10–7–10 fertilizer. Prepare the ground by mixing these thoroughly into the soil. Do this work in the fall and allow it to settle over winter before planting. Many prize-winning onion growers actually roll the soil before planting in the spring to make sure that it is firm at planting time: but that's a luxury. In successive years add the same amount of the same balanced fertilizer at the same rate, as well as forking in a 2–3 in/5–7·5 cm layer of compost or old manure.

Seeding There are two ways you can grow onions—from seeds or from sets. Sets are simply small onions that have been half-grown the year before, then harvested early and stored. Sow seed $\frac{1}{2}$ in/1·3 cm deep at 10–15 seeds per ft/30 cm row. Sow them outdoors around your last frost date in the UK and the Hardy zone of the USA: in Half-hardy and Tender zones sow 6 weeks before your last frost for a spring crop, and again about August for a fall or spring crop. If you're starting from sets put them in the beds 1 week later.

Transplanting Not necessary.

Cultivation Bulbs grow tops in cool weather, and fatten up their bulbs in warm weather. That is what dictates when you plant and when you harvest. However, it's not only temperature that triggers the hormone changes which tell an onion when to bulb. One of the most important factors is daylength. Varieties suitable for growing in the Hardy zone in the USA and through most of Britain are long-day types needing 14–16 hours daylight. Varieties suitable for growing in the Half-hardy and Tender zones are short-day types, needing 12 hours daylight. If you try the wrong types in the wrong zones you'll have them doing all the wrong things at the wrong times: or doing nothing at all. In the Half-hardy and Tender zones what you want is the onions to make topgrowth during the cool fall and winter months, then to start bulbing once the weather warms up in early spring. It's hopeless trying to grow them in those zones through the summer heat. Keep the onions well watered through their growing season. Then withhold water. You can tell when the growing season ends: the tops start turning yellow, then fall over. For extra large onions apply a 4–8–4 liquid fertilizer at fortnightly intervals while the bulbs are making topgrowth.

Harvesting Once the tops start turning yellow you need to do some pre-harvesting work. Go down the rows bending all the topgrowth over. Bend it just above the bulb, and leave it lying flat on the ground.

Always bend the tops away from the sun, so that the bulbs are exposed to all the sunlight they can get. Once the tops have yellowed and shrivelled, lift the bulbs carefully with a fork. Leave them lying on the ground or in wet weather on a paved area for 3–4 days to dry out. Then trim off any straggly roots and trim the tops back. Depending on how you want to store the onions, either trim the topgrowth back to within about 1 in/2·5 cm of the bulb or trim it to about 6 in/15 cm from the bulb. If you trim down to 1 in/2·5 cm, store the onions in a wide-mesh bag hung in the larder or a frost-free shed. If you leave 6 in/15 cm top-growth on, plait the onions together to make an onion string. This can look very decorative hanging in the kitchen. It also means the onions are right to hand when you want to use them.

Mistakes to avoid Planting at the wrong season. Planting in insufficiently prepared ground. Leaving the plants in the ground too long: they will start into growth again.

Shallots	*Varieties*
LATIN NAME *Allium cepa*	'Dutch Yellow'
HARDINESS Hardy	'Giant Red'
pH IDEAL 6·0	
DEPTH TO SOW 1 in/2·5 cm	
WHEN TO SOW Last frost date	
SEEDS PER FOOT 8–12	
DAYS TO GERMINATION 7–14	
% GERMINATION 60	
WHEN TO PLANT OUTDOORS Last frost date	
SPACE BETWEEN PLANTS 2–4 in/5–10 cm	
SPACE BETWEEN ROWS 12–18 in/30–46 cm	
YIELD PER PLANT 8 oz/230 gms	
PLANTS PER PERSON 15	
DAYS TO HARVEST 60–75	
LIFE OF SEED 1 year	

Shallots were for a long time thought to be a distinct onion species, being given the name *Allium ascalonicum*. The specific name is supposed to be a corruption of Ascalon where Richard the Lionheart, who brought this onion back to Britain, defeated the armies of Saladin.

Cytologists now claim the shallot is merely a multiplier variety of the common garden onion. With multiplier onions, instead of planting a single small set and building it up into a great fat bulb, you start with a single small set and finish up with dozens of small bulbs where you planted the set.

Soil Light, sandy, quick-draining and not too rich in nutrients. Plant in a plot manured for a previous crop. If your soil is heavy add in plenty of sand, cinders, perlite or vermiculite to make it lighter. Don't add too much in the way of peat or compost, since this helps retain moisture.

Seeding Don't start from seed. For one thing, shallots very seldom produce any seed for you to start from. Instead start with sets. These are rather smaller than those of the common onion. Plant them around your last frost date. Planting is easy: just push the sets gently into the soil till the tips are at soil level. Do not cover. The sets should be 2–4 in/ 5–10 cm apart where space is short, but up to 10 in/25 cm apart where space permits.

Transplanting Not necessary.

Cultivation Keep weeds down by hand weeding. Don't mulch, which slows down the bulb ripening process, and don't hoe too close to the plants. If you do, chances are you'll either slice the tops off or damage the bulbs. Keep watering to the minimum, but never let the plants dry out while in growth.

Harvesting Lift the bulbs when the tops turn yellow. Use a fork to lift them. You'll probably find that they have grown deeper and spread wider than you expected. Leave the bulbs on top of the rows or in wet weather on a paved surface to dry out. Sort the fat bulbs from the small ones. Save the small ones and replant these in the fall. They will over-winter in the ground and by planting in the fall you'll get next season's crop away to a good start. Wash soil off big bulbs, trim the tops and store as for onions.

Mistakes to avoid Planting sets too deeply. Planting sets too shallowly. Overwatering and/or overfeeding in the hope of getting a bigger crop. You won't: the bulbs will simply rot. Failing to lift mature sets in time. If you leave them in the ground till the freeze sets in they'll lose flavour. If you need to, encourage the bulbs to dry off early by bending the tops over: you may get smaller shallots, but better small ones than none. If you're going to pickle the shallots, do so within a month of harvesting, or they won't have enough flavour left to be worth bothering with.

Leeks	*Varieties*
LATIN NAME *Allium ampeloprasum* var. *porrum*	'Large American Flag'
HARDINESS Hardy	'Malabar'
pH IDEAL 6·5	'Yates Empire'
DEPTH TO SOW 1 in/2·5 cm	'Marble Pillar'
WHEN TO SOW Outdoors: 4 weeks before last frost	'Everest'
Indoors: 8–12 weeks earlier	
SEEDS PER FOOT 8–12	
DAYS TO GERMINATION 7–14	
% GERMINATION 75+	
WHEN TO PLANT OUTDOORS 6 weeks after last frost	
SPACE BETWEEN PLANTS 2–4 in/5–10 cm	
SPACE BETWEEN ROWS 12–18 in/30–46 cm	
YIELD PER PLANT 8 oz/230 gms	
PLANTS PER PERSON 24	
DAYS TO HARVEST 80–90 from sets/130–150 from seed	
LIFE OF SEED 3 years/sets overwinter	

The simplest way to describe a leek is as an onion that does not form a bulb. The part you eat is called the stick. Actually it's the stem (the part between the roots and the leaves). The whole history of the evolution and breeding of the leek has been aimed at making the stick longer and thicker and more tender. That's the whole aim of the tricks of cultivating it too. Just how long, thick and succulent you can get your leek sticks depends on your skill as a gardener. Anyone can grow mediocre leeks: you need to be a good gardener to grow first-rate leeks.

Soil Leeks grow best in a soil that has been manured for a previous crop. They are usually grown in permanent beds, not rotated. Do not manure the soil for the leeks themselves, and do not add artificial fertilizers to the soil—at least not before planting. What leeks like best is a deep, rich, well-worked soil—soil that has been used for generations of vegetable growing being best of all. Good rich loam. If you've got a heavy, clayey soil, lighten it by digging in large quantities of peat or compost, together with sand and cinders. If you've got a very light, sandy soil, make it more moisture-retentive by digging in peat and compost. Prepare the soil in the fall. In spring take out a trench 1 spade wide and 10 in/25 cm deep, throwing up half the soil on each side of the trench. Add a 2–3 in/5–7·5 cm layer of compost to the bottom of the trench, cover that with a 2 in/5 cm layer of soil and set your transplants into that.

Seeding Sow seed out of doors 4 weeks before your last frost date. For an earlier harvest, sow them indoors or under cloches/tents 8–12 weeks earlier. Never sow seed where the plants are to grow. Use a seed bed.

Transplanting Set transplants out 6 weeks after your last frost or as soon as outdoor seedlings are 3 in/7·5 cm tall. When transplanting, make a hole at the bottom of the prepared trench with a dibber and drop the plants into the hole. Do not firm the transplants in the holes; that makes them form bulbs. Set the plants 2–4 in/5–10 cm apart in the trenches: thin to 12 in/30 cm apart in midsummer. Use the thinnings to lace a salad or pep up the flavour of boiled greens.

Cultivation Keep the crop growing well. Keep the trench free of weeds, preferably by hand weeding: hoeing could damage the sticks and weedkillers could damage you. Don't use a mulch to keep the weeds down. Leeks can use plenty of water provided the soil is free-draining. Lack of water will keep the leeks stunted, and they'll be woody when you come to eat them. Add in some tomato liquid feed every other watering, or apply 3–4 oz/sq yd : 87–112 gms/m^2 of 10–7–10 fertilizer in 3 in/7·5 cm bands about 3 in/7·5 cm each side of the plants once they're well into growth. On 1 August put corrugated paper round the sticks, holding it in position with rubber bands or raffia. From then on, start earthing up, using the soil thrown up on one side of the trench. The corrugated paper will start the blanching process and also help to draw the leek. At the same time, clip off half the length of each leaf: this will help to thicken the sticks. Keep on watering and earthing up. Take care when earthing up: any earth that gets into the crown will stay there, no matter how much you wash the leeks.

Harvesting The first sticks should be ready to harvest 3 or 4 weeks before your first frost. Lift them carefully with a fork, again taking care not to get soil in the crown. In Half-hardy areas leeks can stay in the ground and you can go on harvesting them until Christmas. In Hardy areas they should all be out of the ground no more than a month after the first frost.

Mistakes to avoid Overfeeding in the hope of getting bigger, more succulent leeks: it doesn't work. They just rot from the centre outwards, and you don't discover that till you've harvested them. Over-blanching. Don't try to make the stick grow longer than it wants to by earthing up higher than it naturally grows.

Peas

Peas, English, Edible Podded, Snow or Sugar	*Varieties*
LATIN NAME *Pisum sativum*	'Alaska'
HARDINESS Hardy	'Little Marvel'
pH IDEAL 7·0	'Burpee Sweetpod'
DEPTH TO SOW 2 in/5 cm	'Mammoth Metting Sugar'
WHEN TO SOW Last frost date	'Yates Fortune'
SEEDS PER FOOT 6–7	'Kelvedon Wonder'
DAYS TO GERMINATION 6–15	'Onward'
% GERMINATION 80+	'Achievement'
WHEN TO PLANT OUTDOORS —	
SPACE BETWEEN PLANTS 2–3 in/5–7·5 cm	
SPACE BETWEEN ROWS 18–24 in/46–60 cm	
YIELD PER PLANT 1 lb/½ kg	
PLANTS PER PERSON 250–300	
DAYS TO HARVEST 65–90	
LIFE OF SEED 3 years	

Peas have almost certainly been used as food for longer than any other vegetable cultivated today. A native probably of Asia, possibly of parts of Europe, it is known to have been gathered from the wild in prehistoric times. In modern times it has been developed by geneticists and hybridisers to a degree of excellence achieved by no other Old World vegetable. Only corn, America's sole contribution to the basic crops upon which mankind depends, has come further faster. If you are going to grow peas, you need to grow them well, and to do that you need to spend rather more time on them than on most other crops. If you don't like peas, or just don't have the time, skip them and grow something you do have time for. English peas are a cool season crop, ideal for the UK and for the Hardy zone of the USA: in the Half-hardy and Tender zones they are a problem. They can be grown as a spring or fall crop, but they must have 60–70 growing days before the temperatures hit the 70s F/20s C, when they will stop producing.

Soil Peas need an alkaline soil to do well. If you suspect your soil is rather on the acid side, test it and take corrective measures, applying hydrated lime at the recommended rate to lower your pH. Their other main need is plenty of humus but very little nitrogen. The best place to plant them is in ground that has been manured for a previous crop—never plant them in freshly manured ground. They like plenty of moisture at the roots, yet like the soil to be well-drained too, not always the easiest demand to meet. Because of this they are an ideal crop for growing in raised beds, especially since that means you can make up a soil mix designed to meet their soil needs exactly.

Seeding Sow seed 2 in/5 cm deep on or before your last frost date. If you sow them before your last frost date—and it's worth doing because you not only get an earlier crop but can often fit in a fall crop too—cover the seeds with cloches or plastic tents till the seedlings are well up and all danger of frost is past.

Transplanting Not necessary. Peas usually do best sown where they are to grow. However, if you want an early crop you can sow seeds in peat pots, in frames or indoors and then plant them out 4 weeks after your last frost. Shelter them from chilling winds for a further couple of weeks by putting a hessian or burlap screen on the side of the prevailing wind.

Cultivation 2 weeks after planting apply a mulch of compost or peat about 3–4 in/7·5–10 cm deep along the rows. Don't use peat on acid soils—it will only make them more acid. The bush varieties can be grown without staking, but for taller growing varieties you will need to provide some sort of support. Traditional peasticks are increasingly hard to come by and at best are untidy. Rather than spend a fortune getting real peasticks opt for a trellis, just as effective from the peas' point of view and far easier when harvesting time comes from your point of view. Drive stout stakes 5 ft/1·6 m tall into the ground at each end of the row, making sure at least 2 ft/60 cm of the pole goes into the ground. On rows more than 15 ft/5 m long put an extra pole in the

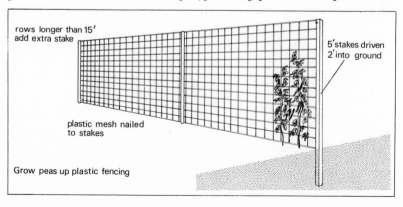

rows longer than 15'
add extra stake

5' stakes driven
2' into ground

plastic mesh nailed
to stakes

Grow peas up plastic fencing

middle of the row. Nail plastic mesh to the poles, and the peas will scramble up this. With traditional peasticks it was usual to plant double rows, with a double row of peasticks. With modern meshes you'll find cultivation and harvesting easier if you only plant a single row on one side of the mesh. It may mean more rows, but you'll get better results that way. Keep the soil moist through the growing season, but never let it become soggy. The mulch should keep the weeds down. Feed at the rate of 3–4 oz/sq yd: 87–112 gms/m^2 with a 6–10–8 fertilizer.

Harvesting Peas are ready to harvest when the pods are well-filled and firm when lightly pressed between thumb and forefinger. They become hard and lose their sweetness if allowed to harden on the plants. If in doubt, pick too early rather than too late. Cut the pods from the haulms: never pull them. Peas are firmly attached to their stalks: if you try to pull the peas you'll probably pull the whole plant out of the ground. Pick the peas low down on the plant first, those higher up later. When the peas have finished cropping, put the haulms and roots into the compost bin: they have a high nitrogen content.

Mistakes to avoid Planting out too early. Though rated as a hardy crop peas can be severely cut back by winds with a high chill factor. They are one of those crops that needs to be kept moving from planting till harvesting, so any conditions like cold snaps which chill the soil will set them back. Take the gamble by all means if you want an early crop: you'll probably get away with it about 5 years out of every 6.

Rootcrops

Beets	*Varieties*
LATIN NAME *Beta vulgaris*	ROOTCROP VARIETIES
HARDINESS Half-hardy	'Boltardy'
	'Empire Vogue'
pH IDEAL 6·5	'Cheltenham Greentop'
	'Burpees Golden'
DEPTH TO SOW 1 in/2·5 cm	'Rulsy Queen'
	'Mono-King Explorer'
WHEN TO SOW Last frost date/under cloches 3 weeks earlier	'Early Wonder'
SEEDS PER FOOT 10–15	
	FOR GREENS
DAYS TO GERMINATION 7–14	'Sugar Beet'
% GERMINATION 60+	'Green Top Bunching'
	'White Beet'
WHEN TO PLANT OUTDOORS —	'Lutz Green Leaf'
SPACE BETWEEN PLANTS 4 in/10 cm	
SPACE BETWEEN ROWS 12–18 in/30–46 cm	

YIELD PER PLANT 8 oz/230 gms

PLANTS PER PERSON 48

DAYS TO HARVEST 50–70

LIFE OF SEED 4 years

Beets are a plant of chalklands surrounding the Mediterranean. The wild plant does not look much like the beets grown today as rootcrops. It looks rather more like the beets grown for greens. The root is not much developed in the wild plant. The swollen root is something that man seems to have encouraged. First records of beets with enlarged roots go back to the sixteenth century, and 150 years ago only one variety had been recorded. Presumably some pretty intensive crop-improving has gone on since then.

Soil In the wild, beets will grow right down their native chalk cliffs and into the seasand. Take a leaf from nature. Give beets a really sandy soil, all the sun they can get and, literally—a pinch of salt. You can grow them in pure sand, but if you want a crop worth harvesting they'll need a little more than that. Plant them in a nutrient-rich soil and they'll split and fork. So just give them sand and humus. Use compost, moss peat, pine needles, anything like that. But no manure. No fertilizer either.

Seeding Sow beet seeds where the plants are to grow. Seed needs to be $\frac{1}{2}$–$\frac{3}{4}$ in/13–18 mm deep in the soil. Sow on your last frost date or 3 weeks earlier under cloches or plastic tunnels.

Transplanting Not necessary.

Cultivation Thin the seedlings to 3–4 in/7.5–10 cm between plants, and 12–18 in/30–46 cm between the rows. Use the thinnings as greens, eating tops, roots and all. Some seed companies sell beet seedballs. If you use these you'll find 3–5 seedlings come up for each seedball you sowed. These should be thinned to 1 plant per seedball as soon as the seedleaves are up. When the beet tops are about 4 in/10 cm high, apply a mulch to keep the weeds down. Feed with a 6–10–18 fertilizer at 2–3 oz/sq yd : 58–87 gms/m². Keep the crop well-watered. It needs a steady supply of moisture through the whole growing season. And it's a crop that needs to grow fast to taste good, so don't slacken up on that watering schedule!

Harvesting Simply dig the beets out of the ground, trim off the tops (excellent material for the compost bin) and wash the earth off. Never scrape the earth off. If you do that you'll damage the skin and the beets will lose flavour.

Mistakes to avoid Planting in rich soils. Irregular watering. Both cause the roots to fork or split. Failure to keep the competition down—and that includes other beets. Weeds and the plants you couldn't quite harden your heart to thin out all compete for moisture at the root. Lack of moisture at the root produces tough, stringy, flavourless beets. You can buy those at the supermarket, so if you're going to grow beets at all you need to do better than that.

Carrots	*Varieties*
LATIN NAME *Daucus carota*	'Red Cored Chantenay'
HARDINESS Hardy	'Nantes'
	'Coreless'
pH IDEAL 6·0	'Autumn King'
DEPTH TO SOW $\frac{1}{4}$ in/6 mm	
WHEN TO SOW Last frost date/again in July for fall crop	
SEEDS PER FOOT 15–20	
DAYS TO GERMINATION 10–21	
% GERMINATION 50+	
WHEN TO PLANT OUTDOORS —	
SPACE BETWEEN PLANTS 1–2 in/2·5–5 cm	
SPACE BETWEEN ROWS 18–24 in/46–60 cm	
YIELD PER PLANT 1–2 oz/29–58 gms	
PLANTS PER PERSON 120	
DAYS TO HARVEST 60–85	
LIFE OF SEED 3 years	

Carrots are native throughout most of Europe, including the British Isles. They seem to have been taken into cultivation at a very early date, and have travelled with Europeans to almost every corner of the earth. They're probably the easiest of all vegetables to grow. They're not fussy about soil pH, not too bothered by the presence or absence of fertilizers (but if you actually want your carrots to fork so you can get a funny picture in the local paper, manure the ground with fresh organic manure as heavily as you can) and they're not much troubled by whether you grow them in a hot climate or a cold climate.

Soil Like all rootcrops, carrots do best in a patch of land that has been manured for a previous crop. Unless you want oddities avoid freshly manured soils.

Seeding Before you sow—unless you buy treated seed—dress the seeds in gamma BHC dust (just shake them around in an envelope containing $\frac{1}{2}$ teaspoonful of the dust). If you don't treat the seeds, don't expect any carrots. Sow seed where plants are to grow. Instead of sowing them in the traditional straight rows, broadcast the seed. Cover seed with not more than $\frac{1}{4}$ in/6 mm soil or sand. Water the seed in. You can sow seed anytime from about 4 weeks before your last frost right up till high summer. Sow seeds in sequences, making each sowing 2 weeks apart.

Cultivation Carrots don't really need cultivating—just harvesting. Keep the soil free of weeds and make sure that the soil they're growing in is always moist, never wet. In wet soils carrots rot. They're the ideal crop for raised beds of specially prepared soil. There you can water them all you like, happily knowing that any surplus moisture will drain away. If you feed them, use only artificial fertilizers. Use a 10–7–10 fertilizer at the rate of 3 oz/sq yd : 87 gms/m² for early crops, use a 6–10–18 fertilizer at 4 oz/sq yd : 112 gms/m² for summer and late crops.

Harvesting In light friable soils just pull the carrots out of the ground by their tops. In heavier soils life them with a lifting fork. Start harvesting when the tops are about 2 in/5 cm high : the carrots will be small and tender. Keep on harvesting till they're starting to get woody, then pull up the rest of that sowing and start harvesting the next sowing. By successional sowing, either in rows or broadcast, you can have carrots for the table from early spring till late fall. Make sure you have all the carrots out of the ground by your first frost. Frost takes the hell out of their flavour. If your carrots get frosted give them to the pigswill man.

Mistakes to avoid Overplanting and underthinning. Also planting in newly manured soils.

Kohlrabi	*Varieties*
LATIN NAME *Brassica oleracea*	'Early White Vienna'
HARDINESS Half-hardy	'Early Purple Vienna'
pH IDEAL 6·5	
DEPTH TO SOW $\frac{1}{2}$ in/1·3 cm	
WHEN TO SOW Indoors: 4–6 weeks earlier	
Outdoors: Last frost date	

SEEDS PER FOOT 8–12

DAYS TO GERMINATION 3–14

% GERMINATION 75

WHEN TO PLANT OUTDOORS 1 week after last frost

SPACE BETWEEN PLANTS 4–6 in/10–15 cm

SPACE BETWEEN ROWS 18–24 in/46–60 cm

YIELD PER PLANT 7 oz/198 gms

PLANTS PER PERSON 20

DAYS TO HARVEST 60–75

LIFE OF SEED 5 years

Kohlrabi is a rarity among vegetables—an interspecific hybrid, a cross between a cabbage and a turnip. No one knows quite when or where the original cross occurred, or whether it was deliberate or not. Not that it matters. It's a first-rate vegetable. It not only tastes good, it actually looks stunning growing in your garden. Tastewise it's a bit like a cabbage and a bit like a turnip but subtler and sweeter than either.

Soil Although the part of a kohlrabi you eat is actually swollen stem not swollen root, and although it sits on top of the soil, not in it, it still counts as a rootcrop. So grow it in soil that has been manured for a previous crop, never in freshly manured soil.

Seeding Sow seed $\frac{1}{2}$ in/1·3 cm deep at, or slightly before, your last frost date. Alternatively sow 4–6 weeks earlier indoors to get an extra early crop. Make successional sowings till midsummer.

Transplanting Plant out seedlings 4–6 in/10–15 cm apart in rows 18–24 in/46–60 cm apart about a week after your last frost. Give protection from winds if necessary. Take care not to set the seedlings too deeply in the ground. If you do the swelling will occur underground and be inedible.

Cultivation Keep weeds down by keeping the hoe moving between the rows: weed between the plants by hand. Be careful if you apply a mulch as a weedsuppressor: you don't want to get it humped up over the swollen part of the stem. Keep the soil moisture level at about 75%. Too dry and the stems will be very woody, too wet and they'll rot.

Harvesting Pull the plants out of the ground. There's no need to dig them out. Trim off roots and leaves. Time to harvest is when the stems

have swollen to almost full size, which is about 4–4½ in/10–11 cm.
Which means the time to harvest is when they are between 3–3½ in/
7·5/9 cm in diameter. Since what you are harvesting is stem, not root,
you'll find that there's a woody core to the kohlrabi. It's hardly notice-
able if you harvest them at the right moment. It becomes more notice-
able the longer you leave them in the ground after the correct moment
for harvesting.

Mistakes to avoid Underthinning, manuring the soil, harvesting too
late.

Radish	Varieties
LATIN NAME *Raphanus sativus*	'Cherry Belle'
HARDINESS Hardy	'Rota'
pH IDEAL 7·0	'French Breakfast'
DEPTH TO SOW ½ in/1·3 cm	'White Icicle'
WHEN TO SOW Last frost date, then every 2 weeks till 1 August	
SEEDS PER FOOT 14–16	
DAYS TO GERMINATION 3–14	
% GERMINATION 75+	
WHEN TO PLANT OUTDOORS —	
SPACE BETWEEN PLANTS 1–2 in/2·5–5 cm	
SPACE BETWEEN ROWS 6–12 in/15–30 cm	
YIELD PER PLANT 1–1½ oz/29–43 gms	
PLANTS PER PERSON 30 per sowing	
DAYS TO HARVEST 20–60	
LIFE OF SEED 4 years	

If your osteopath's told you to stop gardening because you knackered
your back trying to get 3 ft/1 m parsnips out of the ground, try radishes.
They're a first-rate crop, no trouble at all. Give a kid a packet of seeds
and tell him/her to plant them, and you'll still get radishes a *cordon bleu*
cook could make a feast from. Unlike every other rootcrop, radishes do
like a well-manured soil. They only take 3–4 weeks from seed to
maturity—and any plant that grows that fast needs all the molecular
building blocks you can give it. It's a popular vegetable right across the
world today. In some parts it's eaten raw, in others cooked. The only
mystery about it is where it came from in the first place. It is completely

unknown in the wild anywhere in the world. The earliest records of it show that the Egyptians had it established as a staple crop well before the pyramids were built.

Soil Give your radishes a light sandy soil, but work lots of compost into it. At the same time, dig in a 12–6–6 fertilizer at the rate of 2–3 oz/sq yd: 58–87 gms/m². But work it in well and evenly. It's little patches of fertilizer that'll cause the radishes to distort.

Seeding Sow seed $\frac{1}{2}$ in/1·3 cm deep any time from 2 weeks before your last frost onwards. Make successive sowings right on through spring till late summer. Make sowings a week to 10 days apart in spring, at 2 week intervals in summer.

Transplanting Forget it: the crop will have matured before you have time to transplant it.

Cultivation Keep the crop moist at the root from seeding till harvest.

Harvesting Pull the radishes from the ground. Don't wait till they've grown to the full size the catalogues tell you they'll reach: always pluck them a little smaller. If you wait till they are full grown they will have lost some of their crispness. Leave them a little longer and instead of being crisp, they'll be woody.

Mistakes to avoid Overplanting and not harvesting small enough.

Leaf Vegetables

Asparagus

LATIN NAME *Asparagus officinalis*

HARDINESS Hardy

pH IDEAL 6·5

DEPTH TO SOW $1\frac{1}{2}$ in/3·8 cm

WHEN TO SOW 2 weeks after last frost

SEEDS PER FOOT Random

DAYS TO GERMINATION 7–21

% GERMINATION 70

WHEN TO PLANT OUTDOORS 1 week after last frost

SPACE BETWEEN PLANTS 18 in/46 cm

Varieties

'Counover's Colossal'
'Mary Washington'
'Purple Argenteuil'
'Waltham Washington'

SPACE BETWEEN ROWS 36 in/92 cm

YIELD PER PLANT 1½ lbs/665 gms

PLANTS PER PERSON 10

DAYS TO HARVEST 3 years

LIFE OF SEED 2 years

One of those vegetables that most American home gardeners would probably consider a main crop, but most British home gardeners would consider a luxury crop. There are two or three factors which conspire together to deter the British home gardener: asparagus is expensive in the shops, which makes most people think it must either come from a warm climate or else that it is difficult to grow—wrong on both counts. Then it takes 3 years from planting before you can harvest your first sticks: but then that is offset by the fact that if you plant it properly in the first place, you can go on harvesting it for 20 years after that. It also takes quite a lot of space: but then it's so delicious and the cash-saving is so great that this justifies any amount of lawn-grabbing.

Before you even sow the seed or buy the crowns, prepare the soil and prepare it well. Do it thoroughly and you'll have gourmet crops for 15–20 years: do it badly and you'll dig the lot up in disappointment after 5 years.

Here's what you do. Work out the area to be occupied by the asparagus bed. If you're only planting a single row don't forget, asparagus roots can spread as much as 2½–3 ft/75–92 cm each side of the crown, so prepare the row-bed at least 6 ft/2 m wide. Dig the soil deep—to a depth of at least 18 in/46 cm, 24 in/60 cm if your soil is easy to work. Dig in all the compost and manure you can lay your hands on. Let it settle for 6 weeks. Then go over it again, digging in a 10–7–10 fertilizer at the rate of 2–3 oz/sq yd: 58–87 gms/m². Do this work late summer or early fall. Then it's ready to plant come spring.

Seeding Use only fresh asparagus seed. Fresh seed will give you 70%+ germination: 1 year old seed only about 25% germination. Seed more than 2 years old won't germinate at all. Sow 1½ in/3·8 cm deep outdoors, 2 weeks after your last frost. Thin seedlings to 6 in/15 cm apart. Leave in place till the following year.

Plant out If you buy crowns from a garden centre or seed merchant you'll get sticks you can cut 1 year quicker than starting from seed. Make sure you get only male plants: they produce a very much better and heavier crop than female plants. If growing from seed, weed out the female plants. Open up a trench in the ground you have already prepared: it should be 12–18 in/30–46 cm wide and 10 in/25 cm deep. Put

2 in/5 cm well-rotted farmyard manure or compost in the bottom of the trench, making a slight hump in the middle of the trench like a well-cambered road. Sit the crowns on top of the hump and spread the roots well out. Cover the roots with 2 in/5 cm of soil. Do this around your last frost date. If you're planting home-grown seedlings do not try to move them without disturbing the soil on their roots. Shake all the soil off the roots so you can spread them out properly in the prepared trenches. Refill the trenches with the soil you took out of them as the young shoots grow, always letting the shoots keep about 1–2 in/2·5–5 cm above the soil till you have levelled back the trench. Then let them grow away.

Cultivation For best results follow a twice a year feed programme. Use a mixture of organic manure and artificial fertilizer. The fertilizer should be one of the 10–7–10 mixes applied at the rate of 2–3 oz/sq yd: 58–87 gms/m². Make one application before growth starts in spring: make the other as soon as you finish harvesting. This helps the crowns to build up plenty of topgrowth. They need to do that to store enough in their roots to produce a good crop of sticks next year. Keep well-watered and maintain high soil-water levels with a thick mulch.

Harvesting Don't cut a single stick till the plants are 3 years old. The first year you harvest, don't take more than 3 stick from each crown. Let the other shoots grow on. From there on you can cut all sticks from every plant in the bed, provided you know when to stop. First sticks appear within a couple of weeks of the last frost: keep harvesting for 6 weeks then don't cut another stick: let the fern develop. The earliest sticks should be harvested every 3 days. Once in full growth, harvest daily. Harvest when shoots are 6–8 in/15–20 cm tall. Either harvest by bending the spear sharply towards you, or cut it, but if you cut it use a proper asparagus knife otherwise you'll damage oncoming shoots.

Mistakes to avoid Planting too shallowly. Harvesting too soon. Keeping on harvesting too late. Forgetting the watering/feeding programme to build up strength for next season's spears. Easily done when other vegetables seem to demand all your attention.

Celery	Varieties
LATIN NAME *Apium graveoleus*	'Summer Pascal'
HARDINESS Half-hardy	'Golden Self-Blanching
pH IDEAL 6·8	'Greenstick'
DEPTH TO SOW $\frac{1}{4}$ in/6 mm	
WHEN TO SOW 10–12 weeks before transplant date	

SEEDS PER FOOT 8–12

DAYS TO GERMINATION 10–30

% GERMINATION 55

WHEN TO PLANT OUTDOORS 6 weeks after last frost

SPACE BETWEEN PLANTS 8 in/20 cm

SPACE BETWEEN ROWS 24–30 in/60–75 cm

YIELD PER PLANT 3 lbs/1·5 kg

PLANTS PER PERSON 7

DAYS TO HARVEST 100–140

LIFE OF SEED 5 years

Reverses the situation of asparagus: counts as a main crop in Britain (though rather a special one), but hardly grown at all in American home gardens. Probably the main deterrent is the idea that celery is a lot of trouble, all that trenching and earthing up and blanching you heard about at your grandfather's knee. Forget it. Most modern varieties are self-blanching and as easy to grow as cabbage.

Seeding Seed is tiny, so sow it no more than $\frac{1}{8}$–$\frac{3}{4}$ in/3–18 mm deep. Cover flats or pots with newspaper or burlap to prevent rapid drying out. Once seedlings show above soil surface, cover with plastic sheeting held away from the plants with hoops. If sowing in open ground, follow the same practice. Seeds and seedlings need plenty of moisture.

Transplant Plant out seedlings 6–8 weeks after your last frost. By then they should be 2–3 in/5–7·5 cm tall. Handle them carefully: the roots snap easily. Put the seedlings into ground that has been well-fed beforehand. You can work in as much as 3–4 oz/sq yd:87–112 gms/m² of 6–10–18 artificial fertilizer. Work it well into the soil. Celery seedlings will scorch easily if you just leave the fertilizer lying on top of the soil. Since they like a high soil-moisture level it helps if you dig plenty of manure or compost into the ground too.

Cultivation Keep the plants growing well by ensuring high soil moisture content. Mulching with organic materials can help here, reducing evaporation and feeding the plants as well. Modern varieties do not need blanching, but if you want to blanch the plants, here are a couple or three different ways. Either earth them up like white potatoes or plant them in trenches 12–15 in/30–38 cm deep and fill the trenches instead of hilling. Blanching by these methods should start when the sticks are 12–14 in/30–35 cm tall. First gather the leafing tops together and tie them tightly with raffia or thick rubber bands. If you don't do this, earth will get into the heart of the celery and no amount of washing will get it out again. Once the tops are tied, either hill the earth up or fill the trench with soil. There are two quicker, simpler methods that do not involve the risk of getting soil in the heart of the celery. One is to grow the celery from transplant stage to harvesting, straight up through unbaked clay soil drains: the other is to bind the sticks tightly into rolls of cardboard. Allow 2 months for blanching. Harvest plants as needed from one end of the row to the other. Gourmets usually consider that celery needs a touch of frost to perfect its flavour, so expect to start harvesting around your first frost date.

Mistakes to avoid Trying to grow the sticks too tall: earthing up the hills too high or making the trenches too deep. Avoid covering the green, leafy part of the plants when blanching. Never let the plants lack moisture at the roots: lack of sufficient soil moisture is one of the most common causes of stringy celery.

Spinach	*Varieties*
LATIN NAME *Spinacea oleracea*	LONG STANDING VARIETIES (Plant spring)
HARDINESS Hardy	'America'
pH IDEAL 6·5	'White Bloomsdale' 'Long Standing
DEPTH TO SOW ½ in/1·3 cm	'Bloomsdale' 'Giant Thick Leaved'
WHEN TO SOW Hardy areas: 4 weeks before last frost	
Half-hardy and Tender areas: 1 October thro' 1 March	SHORT STANDING (Fall and winter) 'Hybrid No 7'
SEEDS PER FOOT 10–12	'Dixie Market'
DAYS TO GERMINATION 6–14	'Dynamo' 'Viking'
% GERMINATION 60+	
WHEN TO PLANT OUTDOORS —	
SPACE BETWEEN PLANTS 2–4 in/5–10 cm	
SPACE BETWEEN ROWS 12–18 in/30–46 cm	
YIELD PER PLANT 8 oz/230 gms	
PLANTS PER PERSON 5 per planting	
DAYS TO HARVEST 40–70	
LIFE OF SEED 3 years	

Spinach is not the easiest of home garden crops. Few people would pretend it is. It spends most of its time trying to bolt. But read on, because there are several excellent substitutes that are not only easier to grow but probably more palatable too. A native of the Fertile Crescent, spinach itself was grown as a food plant in China long before the West took it up. Now it's grown almost universally throughout the temperate regions of the world. Which suggests that it can be grown successfully, if only you know how. It helps to understand why spinach behaves the way it does. It's an annual, and like most annuals the main purpose of its existence seems to be to produce copious quantities of seed. Which would be all right if we grew it for the seeds instead of the leaves. Once it starts to send up its flowerstalk—that's what's called bolting—production of the useful leaves stops. Bolting is triggered by daylength, and accelerated by low temperatures when the plants are young and high temperatures when the plants are older. The way round this problem is to plant the right varieties at the right season. Choose longstanding (bolting-resistant) varieties for spring sowing, and shortstanding varieties in the fall and in southern areas of the States.

Soil Spinach needs a rich, moist soil, and a position in partial shade may help to slow down the bolting process. Since what you want from spinach is leaf, leaf and more leaf, grow it in a nitrogen-rich soil, preferably one into which plenty of humus in the form of well-rotted manure or compost has been worked, together with a 12–6–6 fertilizer at the rate of 2 oz/sq yd : 58 gms/m².

Seeding Sow seed of longstanding varieties in spring, 4 weeks before your last frost. Then make successional sowings at 10 day intervals till 4 weeks after you last frost. Sow seed of shortstanding varieties in the fall, about 4 weeks before your first frost. In the Half-hardy and Tender zones of the USA sow shortstanding varieties at 2 week intervals from 1 October to 1 March.

Cultivation Keep the weeds down by hoeing: don't mulch. Keep soil moisture content high for spring varieties, not so high for fall varieties, but either way keep the supply even. Feed at the rate of 2 oz./sq yd : 58 gms/m² with a 12–6–6 fertilizer.

Harvesting Leaves are plucked, not pulled. Take the leafstalk between thumb and finger and give it a slight twist at the same time as pulling it downwards and outwards. It should come away cleanly. Keep picking the leaves so long as the plants go on producing succulent ones.

Mistakes to avoid Sowing the wrong type at the wrong season. Sowing too early and too late.

Some Spinach Substitutes
All of these are readily obtainable in America: most can be obtained in
Britain, but are not so well known.

New Zealand Spinach *(Tetragonia expansa)*
This is a first-rate substitute which, once it is better known, may well
become more popular than spinach itself. It is less resistant to cold but
more resistant to heat. It is also valued in many parts of the world because it is comparatively drought-hardy. It forms a low, spreading
ground-cover type plant. Little tendency to bolt. Soil: as for spinach.
Seeding: sow seed 2 weeks after last frost date in Hardy zones, spring
or fall in Half-hardy and Tender zones. The leaves and young stems
can be picked and used just like spinach. The more you pick the more
the plant will produce. Though drought-tolerant, leaves and stems
will be more succulent if you keep the soil moist. Can be harvested
right through the fall into winter from spring sowing.

Malabar Spinach *(Basella alba)*
This is a warm-weather vine, quite unlike any other spinach in its
climbing habit. The leaves are bright green, very glossy. Grows best
in Half-hardy and Tender zones. Sow seed in spring against a fence or
trellis. The growing tips and the young leaves can be harvested and
used like spinach all summer into fall.

Tampala *(Amaranthus gangeticus)*
This is a warm-weather relative of the amaranthus of the flower border.
Several different species are grown as food, either for their leaves or
seeds, mostly in the tropics, but this one, *Amaranthus gangeticus* is the
cream of the spinach substitutes for Half-hardy and Tender zones.
Seed and cultivate as for any common garden annual. The young
leaves are sweeter and tastier than spinach.

Lettuce	*Varieties*
LATIN NAME *Lactuca sativa*	HEAD
HARDINESS Half-hardy	*Crisphead*
	'Avoncrisp'
pH IDEAL 6·5	'Great Lakes'
DEPTH TO SOW ½ in/1·3 cm	
	Butterhead
WHEN TO SOW 2 weeks after last frost, then at 2 week intervals till midsummer	'Webbs Wonderful'
	'Buttercrunch'
	'Arctic King'
SEEDS PER FOOT Head: 4–8	'Iceberg'
Leaf: 8–12	

	LEAF
DAYS TO GERMINATION 4–12	*Leaf or Bunching*
% GERMINATION 80+	'Salad Bowl'
WHEN TO PLANT OUTDOORS 4 weeks after last frost	'Grand Rapids'
	'Oak Leaf'
SPACE BETWEEN PLANTS Head: 12–14 in/30–35 cm	
Leaf: 8–10 in/20–25 cm	*Cos*
	'Dark Green Cos'
SPACE BETWEEN ROWS Head: 18–24 in/46–60 cm	'Paris Island Cos'
Leaf: 12–18 in/30–46 cm	'Histon Crispie'
	'Little Gem'
YIELD PER PLANT 6 oz/170 gms	'Green Cos'
PLANTS PER PERSON 5 per planting	
DAYS TO HARVEST 45–80	
LIFE OF SEED 6 years	

If lettuce is just lettuce to you (and it is to lots of people), then there are one or two little things you ought to know about it before you start trying to grow it. Like there are four different sorts of lettuce. And they belong to two groups. The two groups are: leaf lettuce and head lettuce. Each needs slightly different treatment in the garden. There are two different types in each of those two. Head lettuces are divided into Crispheads and Butterheads. Leaf lettuces are divided into Bunching and Cos types. The head lettuces, as their name suggests, form a tight head rather like a refined cabbage: the leaf lettuces don't have a head, merely a loose gathering together of the leaves. Generally leaf lettuces have a slightly sharper flavour than head lettuces. A lot depends on how you grow them. And grow them you must. They're the mainstay of every salad through the summer season. With a little skill and a couple of frames you can have fresh lettuce straight from the garden the whole year round. Try it.

Soil Lettuces are fussy about the soil they grow in. They like plenty of humus, plenty of moisture and plenty of plant nutrients. However, since they are shallow rooting, there's no point in taking out a 12 in/ 30 cm trench. Only prepare the top 5–6 in/12·5–15 cm of the soil, but prepare it thoroughly. Start in the fall before you intend to grow your first crop by digging all the humus material you can lay hands on into the soil. When you've done that, test its acid reaction. This is particularly important if you've used peat, pine needles or any other acidifying material in the humus build-up. Lettuce likes a pH of 6·5. That's alkaline. More alkaline than most vegetables like. If you find the soil's too acid, lime it to bring it as near pH 6·5 as you can. Test again in early spring: relime if the soil is still on the acid side. All this may seem a lot of trouble to go to for the humble, commonplace lettuce, but it you're going to grow lettuces then grow good lettuces. If your soil is acid, even slightly acid, all you'll grow will be limp, slimy lettuces: the perfect diet for slugs and snails, but not fit for human consumption. A good lettuce is crisp and firm.

Seeding Sow head lettuce seed $\frac{1}{4}$–$\frac{1}{2}$ in/0·6–1·3 cm deep 1 week after your last frost date. Thin to 12–24 in/30–60 cm between the plants, 18–24 in/46–60 cm between the rows. Transplant thinnings. The set-back to growth caused by transplanting will mean you can harvest them later than those left growing. Sow leaf lettuce at the same depth but grow them much closer, thinning to only 3–4 in/7·5–10 cm between plants, 6–12 in/15–30 cm between rows. Re-thin 2 weeks later to 6–10 in/15–25 cm between plants, using thinnings as salad greens.

Transplanting Plant out seedlings 5 weeks later than you sow seed.

Cultivation Lettuce is a quick-growing crop but it must be kept growing on every one of its growing days. The problem is striking the right balance between giving it sufficient water without giving it too much—which merely encourages the plants to rot—and finding the right balance of nutrients. Lettuce is shallow rooting, so water little and often. Never overwater: never soak them. When feeding, avoid high nitrogen content fertilizers. Go for a balanced fertilizer such as a 10–7–10 and apply at the rate of 2 oz/sq yd : 58 gms/m². Sulphate of potash is the one nutrient that will really help you grow lettuces as lettuces should be grown. Apply it in bands down each side of the plants at the rate of 2 oz/ sq yd : 58 gms/m², forked lightly into the soil surface.

Harvesting Just pull the lettuce out of the ground, remove the outer leaves and cut off the worst of the root. Put these trimmings into the compost bin.

Mistakes to avoid Failure to thin sufficiently. This is the cardinal crime when you grow lettuces. Be ruthless about thinning, or you just won't get results. It's simply no good leaving two head lettuce seedlings where there should only be one in the hope of getting two heads. If you get any heads at all they'll be the size of a ping-pong ball: more likely you won't get any heads at all. Similarly with leaf lettuces. The best part for eating is the tender inner leaf-portion. If you leave the rows crowded, all you'll finish up with is a lot of bitter outer leaves.

Swiss Chard (Seakale Beet)	*Varieties*
LATIN NAME *Beta circla*	'Lucullus'
HARDINESS Half-hardy	'Ruby Chard'
pH IDEAL 6·5	'Rhubarb Chard'
DEPTH TO SOW 1 in/2·5 cm	'Fordhook Giant'
WHEN TO SOW Last frost date then at 2 week intervals till July/ August	
SEEDS PER FOOT 6–10	
DAYS TO GERMINATION 7–14	
% GERMINATION 65	
WHEN TO PLANT OUTDOORS —	
SPACE BETWEEN PLANTS 4·8 in/10–20 cm	
SPACE BETWEEN ROWS 18–24 in/46–60 cm	
YIELD PER PLANT 10 oz/283 gms	
PLANTS PER PERSON 5 per planting	
DAYS TO HARVEST 55–75	
LIFE OF SEED 4 years	

Swiss chard or seakale beet is the group name for those beets which are grown for their leaves, and are used as greens, rather than for their roots. The greens are generally used in much the same way as spinach. In the case of varities like 'Ruby Chard' the leaves are a rich ruby colour and look particularly colourful in the vegetable garden with the late-year sun glowing through them.

Soil Like crops grown for their roots, Swiss chard does best in a deeply-worked soil that has been manured for a previous crop. When preparing the soil work in common salt at the rate of 1 oz/sq yd : 29 gms/m² : in the wild, the plant is a coastal strip endemic.

Seeding Sow seed where plants are to grow. Sow the seed 1 in/2·5 cm deep 2 weeks after your last frost and then at fortnightly intervals till July/August. That will give you a succession of crops for roughly 4 months.

Cultivation Keep the soil weed-free, preferably by applying a low-nutrient value mulch such as garden compost. Keep the moisture level of the soil constant: if you try to grow the plants in dry soil the leaves and especially the leaf ribs will be tough and fibrous.

Harvesting Harvest the outer leaves first. This allows the inner leaves to grow on to be harvested later. Always pluck the leaves: never cut them. The correct way to pluck the leaves is to take the stem between forefinger and thumb as close to the rootstock as possible and detach it with a short, sharp downward and outward tug.

Mistakes to avoid Overplanting and underthinning, the usual errors with greens crops. Keep notes your first year of growing this crop to see whether you planted too little or too much.

Fruiting Vegetables

Tomato	*Varieties*
LATIN NAME *Lycopersicon esculentum*	HARDY AREAS
HARDINESS Tender	'Moneymaker'
pH IDEAL 4·0	'Ailsa Craig'
DEPTH TO SOW ½ in/1·3 cm	'Eurocross'
WHEN TO SOW Outdoors: 4 weeks after last frost Indoors: 5–7 weeks earlier	'Maascross' 'Extase' 'Supersonic'
SEEDS PER FOOT Random	'Jet Star' 'Spring Set'
DAYS TO GERMINATION 7–14	
% GERMINATION 75+	HALF–HARDY AREAS 'Homestead'
WHEN TO PLANT OUTDOORS 4–6 weeks after last frost	'Rurgers' 'Manalucie'
SPACE BETWEEN PLANTS 18–36 in/46–92 cm	'Floradel'
SPACE BETWEEN ROWS 36–60 in/1–1·5 m	
YIELD PER PLANT 10–12 lbs/5–6 kg	
PLANTS PER PERSON 1–2	
DAYS TO HARVEST 55–110	
LIFE OF SEED 4 years	

The tomato is a native of the lower Andes, which makes it a warm-season crop. In the wild, the plant is a sprawling, spreading perennial, producing fruits about the size of a good cherry. Cultivated forms are more robust, and are normally grown as annuals. It is probable that no plant has been bred as intensively as the tomato over the last hundred years. You can get varieties with fruits the size of a large apple, red, orange, yellow, smooth-skinned, puckered, ruffled or pear-shaped, oval: there are yellow varieties and 'white' varieties (which are light green) and one of the most recent developments is a race of mini-bush tomatoes suitable for growing in even the tiniest gardens or in a pot on the kitchen windowsill. Whichever type you go for, you'll find tomatoes probably the most exciting and rewarding of all the vegetables in the repertoire. But to grow them successfully, make sure you choose a variety suited to your climate.

Soil This is problem No 1 with tomatoes. They are susceptible to a number of wilts and diseases that are soil borne. The safest way of avoiding these is to grow tomatoes in new soil each season. If you've got raised beds, simply clean them out and fill them with new-bought soilless growing mix. If you're growing tomatoes in the greenhouse, use the peat bale method, planting seedlings direct into plastic-packed bales of peat. Give the soil a good dressing of 6–10–18 fertilizer at the rate of 4–5 oz/sq yd: 112–145 gms/m² or 7–8 oz/sq yd: 198–230 gms/m² under glass.

Seeding If you start tomatoes from seed, the most important thing is to start them early enough. Start them 5–7 weeks before your last frost, and start them indoors. Only start them out of doors in Half-hardy and Tender zones. Seeds need a temperature of at least 60°F/15·6°C to germinate. Sow seed as shallowly as possible, barely covering it. If starting seed indoors, sow in peat pots in a soilless growing mix. Keep humidity around 75%. If you let it get much higher you vastly increase the chances of the seedlings damping off. If it's lower the seedlings will dry out.

Transplanting Many people find it easier to buy in transplants than to raise their own tomatoes from seed. If you decide to do this, make sure you buy your plants as early as possible. Time to set plants out of doors is 4–6 weeks after your last frost. The main criterion is that night temperatures should not drop below 50°F/10°C—which can be tricky in Britain: even in southern counties frost can be recorded on odd nights in almost any month in the year. When buying transplants look for plants with stems about the thickness of a pencil. Go for bushy, compact plants, rather than long, drawn plants. Avoid plants that show any signs of yellowing of the leaves: if you buy them you're buying trouble. Set transplants deeper in the ground than you normally set transplants. The first leaves should be only just above the soil. The part of the stem you bury will sprout extra roots and give the plant more growing and fruiting power.

Cultivation There are two aspects to tomato cultivation: soil management and topgrowth management. The important thing about the soil is that it should be rich in fertilizer and kept at a high moisture content level. Outdoors apply side-dressings of a 6–10–18 fertilizer at the rate of 4–5 oz/sq yd : 112–145 gms/m² at monthly intervals. Double the dose if you're growing under glass. Or feed the plants with a proprietary liquid tomato feed or foliar feed, following the manufacturer's instructions exactly. Topgrowth management depends on the type of tomato you're growing. If you're growing a bush type, just let it grow. If you're growing any of the normal varieties, you'll need to train it. Outdoors, keep the main stem tied to a stake or let the plant scramble over a trellis or lath framework. In the greenhouse, tie a string to a lath fixed across the astragals and take it down to the base of a plant. Then wind it loosely round the stem, and keep winding it as the stem keeps growing. When the plant reaches the top of the string, pinch out the growing tip. Do this for each plant. Both indoors and out, remove all side shoots, keeping the plant to a single stem (except bush varieties). Keep the plants to 5 trusses each. In Britain, when growing tomatoes out of doors, remove any trusses that form after the end of July: they won't ripen and removing them will help to ripen the trusses that have formed earlier. Once fruits start to colour, gradually defoliate the plant, carefully cutting the leaves away from the stem leaving as small a snag as you can. This lets more light get to the fruits, and helps them ripen. Don't defoliate too early: the plants need their leaves to use the energy from sunlight for building good fruit trusses.

Harvesting Trusses ripen from the bottom upwards. You can either remove the fruits as they ripen, or wait till the whole truss is ripe. Either way, cut the fruit or truss from the plant with scissors, don't just pull them away. If growing tomatoes outdoors, remove any trusses that have not ripened fully before your first frost. You can store any fully formed green tomatoes by wrapping them individually in newspaper. Store in a cool place. They'll keep on ripening slowly for another couple of months. Bring stored fruits to a window to finish ripening as needed. After harvesting, uproot the plants and burn them. Don't put them in the compost bin: if they've become infected, that's the surest way there is of spreading the infection to other crops.

Mistakes to avoid Growing a variety unsuited to your area or method of cultivation. Planting out too soon and too late. Defoliating the plants too early.

Eggplant, Aubergine	*Varieties*
LATIN NAME *Solanum melongena*	'Black Beauty'
HARDINESS Tender	'Early Beauty'
pH IDEAL 5·5	'Jersey King'
DEPTH TO SOW ½ in/1·3 cm	'Burpee Hybrid'

LATIN NAME *Solanum melongena*

HARDINESS Tender

pH IDEAL 5·5

DEPTH TO SOW ½ in/1·3 cm

WHEN TO SOW Outdoors: 4 weeks after last frost

Indoors: 7–10 weeks before transplant date

SEEDS PER FOOT 8–12

DAYS TO GERMINATION 7–14

% GERMINATION 60

WHEN TO PLANT OUTDOORS 4 weeks after last frost

SPACE BETWEEN PLANTS 24–36 in/60–91 cm

SPACE BETWEEN ROWS 48 in/1·2 m

YIELD PER PLANT 7 lbs/198 gms

PLANTS PER PERSON 2

DAYS TO HARVEST 80–90

LIFE OF SEED 5 years

This is one of those vegetables that no self-respecting American home gardener would ever be without, but only the most adventurous of British gardeners would attempt. Modern, faster-maturing varieties are making them a more tempting proposition in the UK. Quite a big growing plant, and a bit of a sprawler—a plant that never quite seems to have made up its mind whether to climb or crawl: if you can't find room for it in the vegetable patch, plant it among the ornamentals. It's a showy plant with its big, felted leaves, lavender flowers and brightly coloured fruits. Though low in nutritional value, eggplants are worth growing for their very subtle flavour: no other vegetable has a flavour quite like it.

Soil Eggplants need a light, sandy, sharp-draining soil. If yours isn't naturally like that, dig in plenty of coarse sand, cinders, perlite or vermiculite, as well as some peat and/or compost. If you've got a heavy clay soil all that will achieve is a soakaway effect, with water from all round draining into your carefully prepared eggplant patch: answer— grow your eggplants in raised beds or on small hills if you live on clay soil. Nutrient needs are not high.

Seeding The eggplant is a slow-maturing plant needing the longest growing season you can give it. If you live in a Hardy zone go for the quick maturing varieties. Sow seed indoors $\frac{1}{2}$ in/1·3 cm deep in peat pots so that you can transplant without disturbing the roots. Sow it 7–10 weeks before your plant-out date. Sow outdoors in Half-hardy and Tender zones 4 weeks after your last frost. There's a special way to sow eggplant seed outdoors. Make a groove in the ground 1 in/2·5 cm deep and drop the seed into it. Do not cover the seed. Instead place plastic sheeting over the seed-groove, weighting it down on each side with stones. Heap the soil from the seed-groove up on one side of the groove only so that there will be a slope to the plastic for rainwater to run off freely. If you stretch the plastic level, rain will collect in the middle and press the plastic down onto the seeds.

Transplanting Plant seedlings out in Half-hardy and Tender zones 4–6 weeks after your last frost. Disturb the roots as little as possible when transplanting. Any setback at transplant time delays ripening of the fruit. In Hardy zones, plant out in frames at the same season or pot on into 12 in/30 cm pots and grow in the greenhouse.

Cultivation Only two things you need to remember when cultivating eggplants. The first is that it must have an adequate supply of moisture at all times. The second is that it hates the hoe or any other implement that might disturb its roots. Instead, keep weeds down with a thick mulch of pine needles, shredded pine-bark, peat or even black plastic sheeting.

Harvesting A lot of fuss is made about just when to harvest eggplants. Forget it. It's quite simple. The best eating eggplant fruits are picked when they are between half to three-quarters of the size the catalogues say they'll grow to. Test for ripeness by pressing the side of the fruit gently with the ball of the thumb: if the dent does not spring back the fruit is ready for picking. Other things to look for are a high sheen on the skin; when the sheen's gone dull the flavour will have gone dull too. Learn from experience. Compare what the fruits look like outside before you cut them in the kitchen. Those with brown seeds inside are past eating: you'll usually find that the skin had lost its sheen. Always harvest with pruning shears. The eggplant is a pseudo-shrub, but the stems the fruits grow on are really woody. Handle the fruits gently: they bruise very easily. And never be frightened of picking too many fruits off the bushes: they always produce far more flowers than they can set and convert into fruits. By continuing to harvest you encourage the plants to go on and on producing more fruits.

Mistakes to avoid Setting plants out too early. Wait till the temperatures are up into the 70s F/over 20°C before planting out. Eggplants are very sensitive to chilly weather. It stunts them. Once stunted they never get away again into good fruiting growth.

Peppers, Sweet and Hot	*Varieties*
LATIN NAME *Capsicuum annum* (sweet) *C. frutescens* (hot)	SWEET 'Bell Boy' 'Keystone Resistant Giant' 'Yolo Wonder' 'Fordhook' 'Ruby King' 'California Wonder'
HARDINESS Tender	
pH IDEAL 6·5	
DEPTH TO SOW $\frac{1}{4}$ in/6 mm	
WHEN TO SOW Indoors: 8 weeks earlier Outdoors: 4 weeks after last frost	
SEEDS PER FOOT 6–8	HOT 'Long Red Cayenne' 'Tabasco' 'Hungarian Wax' 'Hungarian Yellow Wax'
DAYS TO GERMINATION 10–25	
% GERMINATION 55	
WHEN TO PLANT OUTDOORS 5 weeks after last frost	
SPACE BETWEEN PLANTS 18–24 in/46–60 cm	
SPACE BETWEEN ROWS 24–36 in/60–91 cm	
YIELD PER PLANT $1\frac{1}{2}$–2 lbs/665–870 gms	
PLANTS PER PERSON 4	
DAYS TO HARVEST 100–120	
LIFE OF SEED 2 years	

The peppers of the vegetable garden are not related botanically to the black and white peppers of the cruet set. They are called peppers because Columbus (Christopher), when he discovered them growing in the Caribbean and brought them back to Europe, described them as more pungent than the peppers of the Old World. Life would have been a little simpler if these had become known as vegetable peppers to distinguish them from the spice pepper. Even then there are two different species of the genus *Capsicum* involved in the vegetable peppers, and you need to know which you are growing not only because they have different culinary uses but also because one needs higher temperatures than the other in the garden. There are sweet peppers, which can be green or red, and there are varieties of *Capsicum annuum*, large growing with a mild flavour. Then there are the varieties of *Capsicum baccatum*, known variously as chillis, pele-pele, capsicums or hot peppers. The fruits of these are much smaller than those of the sweet peppers, and they need hotter summers to grow well. Both are classed as tender, and both are hot weather plants. General cultivation is the same for both. Points to bear in mind when considering whether to grow them or not are these: seed won't germinate at a worthwhile rate under 60°F/15·6°C. The plants will turn yellow, stop growing and never get away again if night temperatures drop below 55°F/13°C. Blossoms will drop (and that means no fruits) if day temperatures drop below 60°F/15·6°C or stay above 75°F/24°C. Again, if the day-time high goes up into the 90s F/over 32°C you'll get blossom-drop. Sounds as though you can't win. You can. So long as they get a day-time maximum temperature around 75°F/24°C and a nighttime maximum around 60°F/15·6°C. The small fruited hot peppers need temperatures higher than the sweet peppers, but, like them, must have a clear-cut day/night temperature differential. Neither type is really successful out of doors in the UK. If you want to grow them there, keep them in 12 in/30 cm pots in a heated greenhouse or large heated frame.

Soil Give peppers a sandy, well-drained soil in the sunniest position you can find. In the Hardy zone try to find them a place where they get reflected heat from a wall or fence.

Seeding By and large you'll get better results by starting with transplants, but if you want to sow seed, sow it indoors 7–9 weeks before transplanting time. Sow the seed shallowly in a soilless growing mix and keep at a temperature of not less than 65°F/18°C.

Transplanting Buy transplants from a reliable garden centre or specialist supplier. Set them in the ground 4–6 weeks after your last frost. Don't hesitate to put a cloche or tent over them if you think the weather's getting too cool for the young plants.

Cultivation Don't disturb the soil round the plants. Keep weeds down with a mulch of compost, old manure, pine needles, shredded bark or whatever is most readily available in your area. Keep the plants moist at the roots but never soak them. As soon as the first flowers appear give the plants a feed. A 6–10–18 fertilizer applied at the rate of 3–4 oz/sq yd: 87–112 gms/m² should be worked into the mulch, then well watered in. Keep on watering from then on. If the plants become dry at the roots they will drop their flowers. Once there are plenty of young peppers on the plant don't worry too much if subsequent flowers drop: it's just nature's way of making sure the plant doesn't overload itself.

Harvesting Always harvest peppers, both the large and the small-fruiting sorts, with pruning shears. Time to harvest is when the peppers change from green to red. Which doesn't help if you're growing a green fruiting variety. No matter: you can harvest peppers at any stage of their development—so don't worry about harvesting them too early. The real waste is harvesting them too late. That's when they start to shrivel and shrink. Your first time round with peppers, leave a couple on the bush and watch their progress through maturity to rotting. It'll cost you two peppers your first year, but you'll be a lot wiser for the rest of your days.

Mistakes to avoid Planting out too early.

Tubers

White Potatoes	*Varieties*
LATIN NAME *Solanum tuberosum*	EARLY
HARDINESS Half-hardy	'Arran Pilot'
	'Irish Cobbler'
pH IDEAL 5·5	'Craig's Royal'
DEPTH TO SOW 4 in/10 cm	'Norchip'
WHEN TO SOW 2 weeks before last frost	MAINCROP
SEEDS PER FOOT 12	'Kennebec'
DAYS TO GERMINATION 7–21	'King Edward VII'
	'Arran Victory'
% GERMINATION 95+	'Dr McIntosh'
WHEN TO PLANT OUTDOORS —	'Katahedin'
SPACE BETWEEN PLANTS 12 in/30 cm	
SPACE BETWEEN ROWS 24–36 in/60–92 cm	
YIELD PER PLANT 6–8 lbs/3–4 kg	
PLANTS PER PERSON 25–30	
DAYS TO HARVEST 90–120	
LIFE OF SEED Overwinter	

White potatoes can be found growing wild all the way from the southern States down through Central America to the southern tip of Chile. First records of them as cultivated crops come from the Andes at high altitudes. Today they are grown throughout the temperate world. In cash terms, they are the most valuable vegetable grown. Surprisingly perhaps, the Soviet Union is the world's largest potato producer. Apart from its food value, the potato is often grown to clean 'dirty' soil—soil infested with perennial weeds. The cultivations involved in growing potatoes, as well as their own peculiar mode of growth, also help to bring soil to a good texture for subsequent crops.

Soil Potatoes will grow in almost any soil. For best results plant them in an acid soil. Avoid soils which have been heavily limed: the crop will be so small it's hardly worth bothering with. They prefer light, sandy soils: in heavy soils they are vulnerable to rots and moulds. If your soil is on the heavy side, make it lighter by digging in plenty of coarse sand, cinders, vermiculite or perlite. There's no need to dig manure into the planting trench, though some humus to help keep moisture levels even is a good idea.

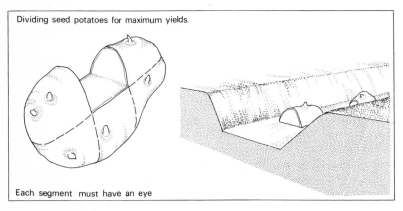

Dividing seed potatoes for maximum yields.

Each segment must have an eye

Seeding Potatoes are only grown from seed by people trying to breed new varieties. You normally buy what are called seed potatoes. There's no mystery about this. They're simply dormant tubers, like dormant dahlia tubers. There are several ways you can deal with your seed potatoes. The simplest is just to plant them 4–6 in/10–15 cm deep where they are to grow. If you want a maxi-crop from a mini-investment, cut the tubers into pieces, making sure that there is one eye (sprouting bud) on each piece and plant the pieces. If you want an extra early crop, start the tubers indoors before planting out. Do this by laying them on flats of damp peat in a temperature of about 55°F/12°C. Plant out pre-sprouted tubers when the shoots are 4 in/10 cm long. The usual time to plant out potatoes is on your last frost date. You can produce earlier crops by growing them entirely under frames, but they're a space-consuming vegetable and there are other vegetables that will better reward your efforts in the frame.

Transplanting Not applicable.

Cultivation The seed potato you planted will grow in two directions simultaneously. It will send roots down below itself and at the same time it will send shoots upwards. From the cropping point of view it is these upgrowing shoots that matter. As they shoot up through the soil, roots will grow laterally from them, and it is these roots that will produce the potatoes you harvest. By harvest time, the original potato you planted will have withered and died. Cultivation is aimed at encouraging the potato to produce long shoots above the seed tuber, since the longer the shoots, the more side roots and so the more new potatoes you'll get. This encouragement is given by earthing up the rows. In the UK this is usually done by continuous ridging—building hills in straight rows up to 12 in/30 cm high at planting time. In the USA the first earthing up is done when the shoots are about 3 in/7·5 cm out of the ground. Soil should be heaped round the shoots so that only the green growing tips show. Earth up again a fortnight later, and again a fortnight after that. By that time you should have hills about a foot/30 cm high along the rows. If you find earthing up a bore, pack light, strawy compost or very old manure round the shoots: it'll produce the same results. Orientate the rows north/south to give the crop maximum light.

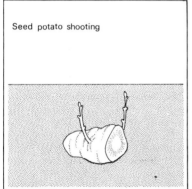
Seed potato shooting

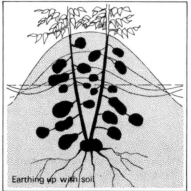
Earthing up with soil

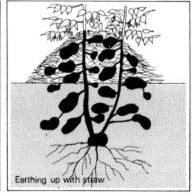
Earthing up with straw

Harvesting The time to harvest white potatoes is when the leaves start to turn yellow. Don't wait till they have died off completely. Lift the potatoes by placing a fork in the ground at a little distance from the visible leaves and levering the soil gently loose. Turn the soil several times, picking out the fresh tubers from the soil as you do so. After harvesting, level the land and burn the old haulms. Don't compost them: it's a sure way to start and spread fungal infections.

Mistakes to avoid Trying to grow potatoes in heavy, wet soils. Letting the new tubers become exposed to sunlight: this turns them green. A green potato is a poisonous potato. It probably won't kill you if you eat it, but it could make you feel ill enough to wish it had.

Appendix

Conversion tables for British and Metric Weights and Measures
The figures in the central of the three columns in each table
represent either one or the other of the two side columns, as
required, e.g. 1 kg = 2.205 lb, 1 lb = 0.454 kg, 100 ha = 247.105 ac,
100 ac = 40.469 ha.

Kilograms	*Weight* kg or lb	Pounds	Hectares	*Area* ha or ac	Acres
0.454	1	2.205	0.405	1	2.471
0.907	2	4.409	0.809	2	4.942
1.361	3	6.614	1.214	3	7.413
1.814	4	8.819	1.619	4	9.884
2.268	5	11.023	2.023	5	12.355
2.722	6	13.228	2.428	6	14.826
3.175	7	15.432	2.833	7	17.297
3.629	8	17.637	3.237	8	19.769
4.082	9	19.842	3.642	9	22.240
4.536	10	22.046	4.047	10	24.711
9.072	20	44.092	8.094	20	49.421
13.608	30	66.139	12.140	30	74.132
18.144	40	88.185	16.187	40	98.842
22.680	50	110.231	20.234	50	123.553
27.216	60	132.277	24.281	60	148.263
31.752	70	154.324	28.328	70	172.794
36.287	80	176.370	32.375	80	197.684
40.823	90	198.416	36.422	90	222.395
45.369	100	220.462	40.469	100	247.105

1 lb = 16 ounces (oz)
1 hundredweight (cwt) = 112 lb
1 acre = 4840 sq yards

	Weight/area	
	kg/ha	
kg/ha	or lb/ac	lb/ac
1.121	1	0.892
2.242	2	1.784
3.363	3	2.677
4.484	4	3.569
5.605	5	4.461
6.726	6	5.353
7.848	7	6.245
8.969	8	7.138
10.090	9	8.030
11.211	10	8.922
22.421	20	17.844
33.632	30	26.766
44.843	40	35.688
56.054	50	44.609
67.265	60	53.531
78.486	70	62.453
89.696	80	71.374
100.907	90	80.296
112.108	100	89.218

Conversion tables for British and Metric Weights and Measures

The figures in the central of the three columns in each table
represent either one or the other of the two side columns, as
required, e.g. 1 cm = 0.394 in, 1 in = 2.540 cm, 1 m = 1.094 yd,
1 yd = 0.914 m.

Length

Centi-metres	cm or in	Inches	Metres	m or yd	Yards
2.540	1	0.394	0.914	1	1.094
5.080	2	0.787	1.829	2	2.187
7.620	3	1.181	2.743	3	3.281
10.160	4	1.575	3.658	4	4.374
12.700	5	1.969	4.572	5	5.468
15.240	6	2.362	5.486	6	6.562
17.780	7	2.756	6.401	7	7.655
20.320	8	3.150	7.315	8	8.749
22.860	9	3.543	8.230	9	9.843
25.400	10	3.937	9.144	10	10.936
76.200	30	11.811	27.432	30	32.808
101.600	40	15.748	36.576	40	43.745
127.000	50	19.685	45.720	50	54.681
152.400	60	23.622	54.864	60	65.617
177.800	70	27.559	64.008	70	76.553
203.200	80	31.496	73.152	80	87.489
228.600	90	35.433	82.296	90	98.425
254.000	100	39.370	91.440	100	109.361

1 yd = 3 feet = 36 inches

Litres	*Volume* l or gal	Gallons
4.546	1	0.220
9.092	2	0.440
13.638	3	0.660
18.184	4	0.880
22.730	5	1.100
27.276	6	1.320
31.822	7	1.540
36.368	8	1.760
40.914	9	1.980
45.460	10	2.200
90.919	20	4.400
136.379	30	6.599
181.839	40	8.799
227.298	50	10.999
272.758	60	13.199
318.217	70	15.398
363.677	80	17.598
409.137	90	19.798
454.596	100	21.998

1 gal = 8 pints

Index